The LAIRD *of* FORT WILLIAM

The LAIRD *of* FORT WILLIAM

William McGillivray
and the North West Company

IRENE TERNIER GORDON

VICTORIA · VANCOUVER · CALGARY

Heritage House Publishing Company Ltd.
heritagehouse.ca

LIBRARY AND ARCHIVES CANADA CATALOGUING IN PUBLICATION

Gordon, Irene Ternier, author
    The Laird of Fort William: William McGillivray and the North West Company / Irene Ternier Gordon.

Issued in print and electronic formats.
ISBN 978-1-927051-72-6 (bound).—ISBN 978-1-927051-73-3 (epub).—
ISBN 978-1-927051-74-0 (pdf)

    1. McGillivray, William, 1764-1825. 2. Fur traders—Canada—Biography. 3. Businessmen—Canada—Biography. 4. Politicians—Canada—Biography. 5. North West Company—Biography. 6. Scots—Canada—Biography. I. Title.

FC3212.1.M45G67 2013   971.03   C2013-903385-8   C2013-903386-6

Edited by Lesley Reynolds
Proofread by Lesley Cameron
Cover and book design by Jacqui Thomas
Cover images: *Portrait of William McGillivray*, Library and Archives Canada,
    Acc. No. 1956-7-1, C-000167 (front); *Fort William*, ca. 1811, watercolour by Robert Irvine,
    Peter Winkworth Collection of Canadiana, Library and Archives Canada,
    Acc. No. R9266-290, C-151675 (front); painting titled *Montreal from the Mountain*,
    by James Duncan, shows Château St. Antoine, the McGillivray country estate,
    McCord Museum M966.61-P2 (back).
Frontispiece photo: William and Magdalen McGillivray, their daughter Anne, and pets in an
    1806 portrait by William Berczy, McCord Museum M18683.

 This book was produced using FSC®-certified, acid-free paper, processed chlorine free and printed with vegetable-based inks.

Heritage House acknowledges the financial support for its publishing program from the Government of Canada through the Canada Book Fund (CBF), Canada Council for the Arts, and the province of British Columbia through the British Columbia Arts Council and the Book Publishing Tax Credit.

| Canadian Heritage | Patrimoine canadien | The Canada Council for the Arts | Le Conseil des Arts du Canada | BRITISH COLUMBIA ARTS COUNCIL |

17 16 15 14 13 1 2 3 4 5

Printed in Canada

—≡:≡—

*Dedicated to representatives of the four present-day
generations of the McGillivray family who are directly
descended from William's son Simon:
Sylvia Hansen (née McGillivray),
Lisa Hansen,
Felix Gordon,
and Amelia Hansen*

—≡:≡—

⇒ CONTENTS ⇐

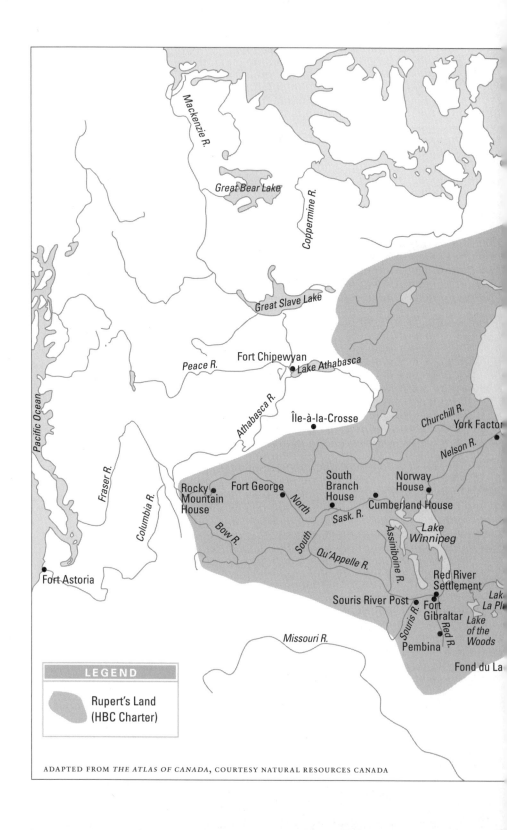

LEGEND

Rupert's Land
(HBC Charter)

Mackenzie R.

Great Bear Lake

Coppermine R.

Great Slave Lake

Peace R.

Fort Chipewyan
Lake Athabasca

Athabasca R.

Pacific Ocean

Île-à-la-Crosse

Churchill R.

York Factor

Nelson R.

Fraser R.

Columbia R.

Rocky Mountain House

Fort George

North

South Branch House

Sask. R.

Norway House

Cumberland House

Bow R.

South

Qu'Appelle R.

Assiniboine R.

Lake Winnipeg

Fort Astoria

Souris River Post

Souris R.

Fort Gibraltar

Red River Settlement

Lake La Pl

Lake of the Woods

Missouri R.

Pembina

Red R.

Fond du La

ADAPTED FROM *THE ATLAS OF CANADA*, COURTESY NATURAL RESOURCES CANADA

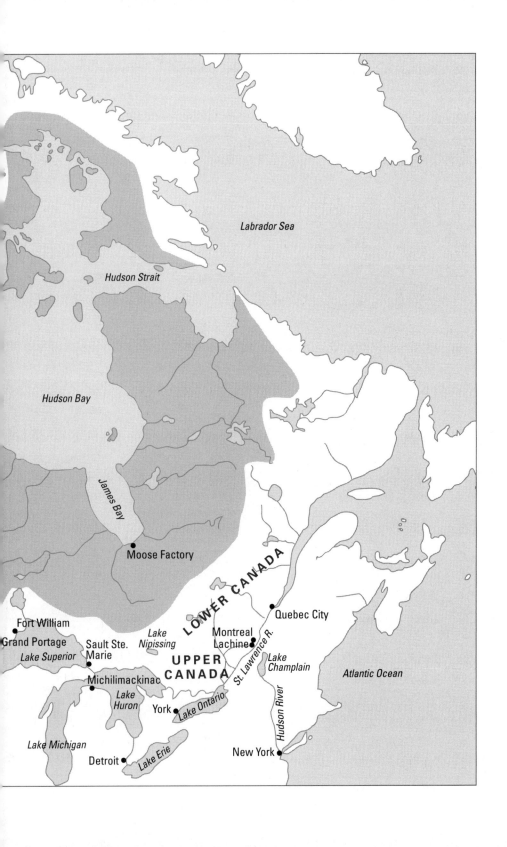

Labrador Sea

Hudson Strait

Hudson Bay

James Bay

Moose Factory

LOWER CANADA

Fort William

Grand Portage

Lake Superior

Sault Ste.
Marie

Lake
Nipissing

Quebec City

Montreal
Lachine

St. Lawrence R.

UPPER
CANADA

Lake
Champlain

Atlantic Ocean

Michilimackinac

Lake
Huron

York

Lake Ontario

Lake Michigan

Lake Erie

Detroit

Hudson River

New York

PREFACE

It was the dream of the clerk to become the master of a trading post; the trader aspired to become a winter partner; the winter partner braved toil and privation for a decade in the hope of spending his declining years in ease and luxury as a Montreal bourgeois. The price of promotion was obedience and success. No system could have been devised more effectively to stimulate ambition [and] to remove inconvenient scruples . . . For keen, hard, shrewd efficiency the NWC was perhaps the most terribly effective organization that had ever arisen in the New World.

⇒ CHESTER MARTIN ⇐

Highly regarded Canadian historian Chester Martin wrote the above comments about the North West Company in 1916. The company is now merely part of the romance and colourful lore of Canadian fur-trade history. In its heyday, however, it was an economic powerhouse, run by British North America's new merchant aristocracy —many of whom were Highland Scots. Chief among those men was William McGillivray.

I first became interested in writing a biography of William McGillivray when I discovered my indirect connection to him through my grandson Felix. Felix's maternal grandmother is a McGillivray who is directly descended from William. This makes Felix a six or seven times removed great-grandson to William. But I had another reason for telling the story of William McGillivray. Although he was the wealthiest and most powerful businessman in British North America in the early years of the nineteenth century, particularly during the decade between 1804 and 1814, he is not well known today. The only biography ever written about him was published in 1962 and updated about ten years later.

In the course of doing my research for this book, I visited many places connected to the McGillivray family, including Dunlichity, in the Scottish Highlands near Inverness, where William McGillivray grew up, and Pennyghael on the Isle of Mull, where he bought the estate to which he had hoped to retire after his fur-trading days were over. These two places have changed surprisingly little in the last two centuries. There are far more cows and sheep in the area than people. The Dunlichity church, rebuilt in 1758, still exists, as does the cemetery where William's parents are buried. The church is still used occasionally for weddings, baptisms, or funerals. Pennyghael is a small village on the Isle of Mull in the Inner Hebrides. Unfortunately, Pennyghael House, though still standing, has fallen into ruin. Because it is not on a public road, I was unable to see it.

I also visited two places closely connected to the Highlanders and the Jacobite cause they supported: Prestonpans, on the outskirts of Edinburgh, site of a 1745 Jacobite victory over the forces of King George II; and Culloden Moor, where the Jacobite cause and many Highlanders met a final, brutal end in 1746.

Places in modern Canada with McGillivray connections have changed much more. Montreal's population rose from 9,000 people in 1800 to 1.6 million in 2011, while Sault Ste. Marie's population is now over 79,000 citizens. The city of Thunder Bay has grown up near the site of Fort William, which has been recreated as the Fort William Historical Park. William McGillivray never travelled farther west than Fort William after the mid-1790s and therefore never saw even the beginnings of any western Canadian cities. Despite this, the Montreal-based McGillivray was arguably the richest and most influential businessman in British North America during the early years of the nineteenth century and can truly be regarded as one of Canada's first entrepreneurs.

A HIGHLAND TRAGEDY

Rise, rise! Lowland and Highlandman,
Bald sire to beardless son, each come and early;
Rise, rise! mainland and islandmen,
Belt on your broad claymores—fight for Prince Charlie;

When hath the tartan plaid mantled a coward?
When did the blue bonnet crest the disloyal?
Up, then, and crowd to the standard of Stuart,
Follow your leader—the rightful—the royal!

JOHN IMLAH
FROM "THE GATHERING," TRADITIONAL SCOTTISH SONG

As morning dawned on April 16, 1746, the exhausted, hungry, and demoralized Jacobite forces led by Prince Charles Edward Stuart, known as Bonnie Prince Charlie, rested on the cold ground of Culloden Moor, near Inverness. Seven months earlier, the Jacobites—mostly Highlanders—had achieved a stunning and unexpected victory over British forces at the Battle of Prestonpans, near Edinburgh. But the victory had not led to the hoped-for restoration of the Stuart prince to the British throne. After an aborted invasion of England, the Jacobites had withdrawn to the north of Scotland.

As the Highlanders slept in the heather, the Duke of Cumberland led some nine thousand soldiers toward Culloden. Around 8 AM, Jacobite commander-in-chief Lord George Murray and Prince Charlie learned of Cumberland's imminent attack and organized a defensive line. The Highlanders caught sight of Cumberland's army at around 11 AM, and by 1 PM the two armies were face to face. Unfortunately for the Highlanders, Culloden Moor was flat and much more suited to English cannons than the traditional Highland charge, which relied on the Highlanders taking a stand on high ground above the opposing force. In order to inflict maximum damage, the British used grapeshot instead of cannonballs. Each time they fired, forty or fifty grapeshot hurtled toward the Highlanders instead of a single cannonball, killing or wounding many more men at a time.

Cumberland continued to bombard the Highlanders without advancing. Finally Prince Charlie ordered his forces to attack. The first regiment to respond was Clan Chattan, led by young Alexander McGillivray, who had taken command of the clan when its senior leader, the chief of the MacIntoshes, had refused to get involved in what he saw as a hopeless cause. The Chattan charge was a fearsome spectacle. Crowds of clansmen ran at top speed toward the English forces, yelling their clan war cries and waving broadswords, shields, and dirks. In order to avoid a boggy area, Clan Chattan veered to the right onto a road that crossed the moor. This caused great confusion to the Highland regiments to their right, who were pushed toward a wall. Adding to their difficulties, the wind was in the Highlanders' faces. Lashed by rain, sleet, and choking smoke from Cumberland's cannons, they could scarcely see or breathe.

Such terrible losses were inflicted on the Highlanders that orders were quickly given for them to fall back and leave the field. Between 1,000 and 1,200 Highlanders were killed, while only about 300 of Cumberland's men were killed or wounded. Cumberland's men slaughtered so many wounded Jacobites after the battle was over that he would be forever known to the Highlanders as "The Butcher." He then led his force to Inverness, where the men raped and pillaged. A local minister described Cumberland's soldiers as "uncontrollable and vicious."

Following the Battle of Culloden, the last battle fought on British soil, Charles Edward Stuart fled and soon escaped to France. Some of the Highlanders tried to regroup shortly after the battle but gave up when they learned the prince had abandoned them.

The Well of the Dead at Culloden Moor marks where the chief of the McGillivray (sometimes spelled MacGillivray) clan fell during the 1746 battle that decimated many of the Highland clans.
IRENE TERNIER GORDON

The defeat at Culloden was catastrophic for many Highland clans, but none more so than the McGillivrays, the McTavishes, and the Frasers. Because many Highlanders were Jacobite supporters, a punitive crackdown was launched against them following their defeat at Culloden. The Act of Proscription forbade the wearing of any type of Highland dress, including tartan and kilts. Only those serving in Highland regiments were allowed to wear the tartan. That act was followed by the Heritable Jurisdictions Act, which forced all Scottish landowners to accept English jurisdiction or forfeit their land. Those landed peers who participated in the '45 uprising had already lost their land to the English. A final law passed in 1747 weighed especially heavily against the McTavish and Fraser clans. It stated that "all the King's subjects in Great Britain should be pardoned of every treasonable offence against the State committed by them before the 15th of June in that year, with the exception of John McTavish, Simon Fraser of Lovat, and several other Notables."[1]

As a direct result of the crackdown on the Highlanders after Culloden, tens of thousands of them emigrated to the New World after deciding that they had no future in Scotland. The fur trade, a major employer in British North America, appealed to many Highlanders, who came from wild country and were accustomed to hunting and fishing as part of their traditional way of life.

1 FAMILY TIES: THE McGILLIVRAYS AND McTAVISHES, 1764–76

My love to the warlike race,
The gentle, vigorous, flourishing.
Active, of great fame, beloved,
Whom we have over us,
The race that will not wither, and has descended
Long from every side,
Excellent McGillivrays of the Doune,
Whom I shall ever hold in esteem.

JOHN DONN M'JAMES V'DAVID GAELIC LAMENT
FOR THE McGILLIVRAYS SLAIN AT CULLODEN FROM
"SONG TO McGILLIVRAY OF DUNMAGLASS"

Clan McGillivray is part of a confederation of clans known as Clan Chattan, which dates back to 1268. That year, Gillivray, a direct descendant of a Viking king, allied himself with the chief of Clan Mackintosh at Inverness Castle. The McGillivray clan seat was in the western Highlands at Dunmaglass on the eastern shore of Loch Ness near Dunlichity, where William McGillivray was born in 1764. He was the eldest of eight children born to Donald Roy McGillivray (1741–1803) and Ann McTavish (1741–1807).

Donald McGillivray was a tacksman on the Fraser of Lovat estate. Traditionally, the chief of each clan leased out parcels of his land to men, often his relatives, who could be considered the nobles or middle managers of the clan. Known as tacksmen, these men, in turn, sublet the land to other tenants and subtenants. The tenants worked the land and sometimes provided military service. The tacksman was obliged to provide the chief with goods and labour, along with armed men if required.

Many tacksmen—the most educated and entrepreneurial people in Highland society—emigrated or moved elsewhere in Scotland following the Battle of Culloden, sometimes taking all their tenants with them. Landlords had discovered that they could make more money grazing sheep than renting their land to tenants. Between 1763 and 1773, about ten thousand people left the Highlands in the first stage of the Highland Clearances. Because Donald McGillivray was a tacksman, the family considered themselves above the common folk. Nevertheless, they were so poor that they could not afford to send their children away to school. Before 1700 there were very few schools in the Highlands; but by 1772, when William was eight years old, there were 159 free schools where children would be given a minimal education in reading, writing, and arithmetic "with such other subjects as should be considered suitable to the pupil's circumstances."[1] However, there was little or no money to pay a teacher. In addition, most of the school buildings were extremely poor and comfortless. The wind and rain whistled through the dry stone or turf walls, and the windows were frequently without glass. The roofs were covered with turf divots and broom (twigs) or bracken and often leaked. The only heat was provided by a small peat or wood fire built directly on a floor of bare earth. It is likely that William and his brothers attended such a school as soon as they were old enough.

Two popular pastimes during William's schooldays were shinty, a game similar to field hockey, and cockfights. As shocking as the idea of cockfights is to most modern North Americans, they were common occurrences in Highland schools and took place whenever a boy was able to get a cock to take to school. One or both birds were often wounded or killed in the fight, and the teacher kept these to augment his meagre diet.

William McGillivray's life might have followed a very different course were it not for his uncle, the enterprising Simon McTavish. The McTavish

William McGillivray attended Dunlichity church as a child, and his parents were buried there.
IRENE TERNIER GORDON

family had arrived in the Highlands early in the sixteenth century and settled at Garthbeg, near Inverness. Simon's father, John McTavish (ca. 1702–74), married Mary Fraser (ca. 1716–70) of neighbouring Garthmore. John and Mary became the parents of eight children, including Ann, Elizabeth, and Simon. Although John McTavish was in hiding or in North America during the ten years following the defeat at Culloden, he must have been home occasionally because his wife gave birth to four children between 1748 and 1753.

Simon McTavish grew up on stories about the glory of Prestonpans and the tragedy of Culloden. He was born only four or five years after these battles that had such a profound effect on his family. As a direct result of his participation in the Battle of Culloden, Simon's father was forced to spend many years away from his family. In January 1757, he was commissioned a lieutenant in a military unit led by his kinsman Lieutenant Colonel Simon Fraser of Lovat. Fraser evidently formed this military unit, which would become well known as the 78th Fraser Highlanders, in order to receive a pardon from the British government. John McTavish went to

North America with the Fraser Highlanders in 1759 and fought at the Battle of Louisburg before returning home in 1761 or 1762.

Simon McTavish left the Highlands for North America at the age of 13—the year his nephew William was born to Ann and Donald McGillivray—with his newly married sister Elizabeth and her husband, Hugh Fraser. In 1764, they settled at Johnstown, the estate of Sir William Johnson in the Mohawk Valley of today's New York State. Johnson, who was the largest landowner and most influential citizen of the Mohawk Valley, encouraged people from Ireland and the Scottish Highlands to settle on his land as tenant farmers or indentured labourers. In effect, Johnson took over the role of the clan chieftain. He traded in agricultural products and furs, becoming wealthy through the fur trade.

Johnson died shortly before the American Revolution began, and his son, Sir John Johnson, inherited the estate. When Revolutionary troops invaded the estate, Sir John and most of his tenants fled to Montreal, where Johnson raised a Loyalist regiment. Many of the people Sir William had helped immigrate to North America, like Simon McTavish, would later play important roles in the Canadian fur trade.

Simon, who had soon decided that he was not suited to farming, left Johnstown before the American Revolution broke out. In 1766, he began training for the business career that would make him one of the wealthiest men in British North America before the close of the eighteenth century. He first went to work for Commodore Alexander Grant, who was in charge of British naval vessels on the Great Lakes. Because private shipping was almost non-existent at that time, commercial goods were allowed as cargo on Crown ships. Since Grant controlled cargo space on these ships, he was at the hub of the commercial network between Detroit and New York. After 1768, Grant monopolized all shipping on the Great Lakes.

In about 1772, McTavish went into business with his close friend William Edgar, an important Detroit merchant. Two years later, in partnership with James Bannerman, McTavish established the first of many fur-trade companies to which he was connected over his lifetime.

When Simon left home in 1764 he was a penniless 13-year-old boy with little education. When he returned in triumph on his first visit home to Scotland in the fall of 1776, he was a wealthy man-about-town—at least in the eyes of his relatives. Great excitement abounded in the home of Ann and Donald McGillivray when they learned that Simon was coming to visit. The McGillivray children had grown up hearing stories of the family's history as proud Scottish Highlanders and Jacobites, but they had also heard many tales of life in North America as recounted in letters from their mother's sister and brother, who had immigrated there the year William was born.

The beautifully dressed Simon kept his family spellbound with tales of hunting, of trading for beaver pelts with the Native people, and of wilderness canoeing with voyageurs to places with exotic names like Michilimackinac and Sault Ste. Marie. To his impoverished relatives, the fifteen thousand pounds Simon had earned by selling his furs in London was a huge fortune. He offered to use some of his money to pay for his nephews to go away to school and likely at this time also promised to give the boys jobs in North America once they finished their education. Thus, Simon's visit would have a profound effect on the lives of young William and his brothers.

2 THE BIRTH OF THE NORTH WEST COMPANY, 1774—84

I voyage north, I journey south,
I taste the life of many lands,
With ready wonder in my eyes
And strong adventure in my hands.

I join the young-eyed caravans
That storm the portals of the West;
And sometimes in their throng I catch
Hints of the secret of my quest.

In the lone cabin, sheathed in snow,
I bide a season, well content,
Till forth again I needs must fare,
Called by an unknown continent.

CHARLES G.D. ROBERTS
FROM "THE VAGRANT OF TIME"

About the time McTavish made his first visit home to Scotland, two events occurred that would greatly influence his subsequent career: the American Revolution and the passing of the Quebec

Act. The Quebec Act, which became effective in May 1775, enlarged the boundaries of Quebec to include Labrador and the so-called Indian Territory south of the Great Lakes between the Mississippi and Ohio Rivers. While most residents of Quebec were naturally pleased with the territorial expansion, colonists in what would soon become the United States were enraged because they considered the Indian Territory theirs by right.

Other terms of the Quebec Act stipulated that Quebec was to be governed by a governor and appointed council and that its legal system would be a combination of French civil law and British criminal law. Anglophone residents were unhappy that they would not have an elected assembly, and some objected to being under French civil law.

McTavish wrote to William Edgar from New York on December 24, 1774, with concerns about the passage of the Quebec Act. He said that merchant Isaac Todd was delegated by the Montreal merchants to prepare petitions begging for the repeal of the act. He believed that it would "be of infinite hurt" to the fur trade, and that even if they were successful in having the act repealed, they would not have the news before July or August. "In the mean time," he asked, "what are we to do for rum?"[1] Because the act would not let them bring supplies from New York, they would be forced to break off that connection and get their supplies from Canada.

Then the young McTavish turned from weighty business matters to asking his friend Billy for the latest gossip from Detroit and recounting his own adventures in New York:

> For my part, I am now here in the land of good cheer viz good wine, good oysters, and pretty girls; tho' people in general discourage all kind of dissipation . . . On this account we have no plays; and decency prevents my dancing, as I received the news of my father's death . . . I need not wish you a Merry Christmas for I dare say you'll make it so. For my own part, I'll go very solemnly to church and Detroit shall be remembered in my prayers, as I believe few of you pray for yourselves.[2]

Many colonists considered the Quebec Act one of the "Intolerable Acts" that contributed to the outbreak of the American Revolution. In the fall of 1775, two American armies marched north in an attempt to take control of Canada. Montreal quickly fell. The siege lasted until spring, when the British sent a fleet up the St. Lawrence and the Americans retreated. The initial disapproval felt by many influential English-speaking Montreal merchants toward the Quebec Act changed as the fighting went on. With the Americans now excluded from the fur trade with Britain, the Montreal merchants thrived.

McTavish spent the winter of 1775–76 at Detroit, which was well supplied with trade goods. The American Continental Army occupied Montreal over the winter, so the Montreal traders were unable to get their goods to Grand Portage, their major fur-trade depot on Lake Superior, in the summer of 1776. As a result, McTavish had little competition and traded for many more furs than normal, marketing beaver pelts worth fifteen thousand pounds on his trip to London the following winter.

In mid August of 1776, McTavish wrote to Edgar, "Dear Billy, Our bad success at Detroit has been in some measure made up by my jaunt to the carrying place [Grand Portage]. We can say with a heartfelt satisfaction that this fall we can pay every one their own." As usual, he ended his letter on a personal matter, "I can't say whether we have got the £20,000 prize or not, not even if the tickets have been purchased on our account."[3] Obviously, lotteries are not something new.

On October 4, McTavish wrote a final letter to Edgar about his proposed London trip:

> Dear William . . . Don't you think I will be able to swagger and strut . . . when I'll come from London! I believe I shall. It must give a man an air of importance to have been there, and it leaves a person . . . [able] to tell many fine stories of himself—which none of you poor bearskin catchers can contradict. To be serious . . . I am damnably afraid I shall repent of my jaunt if peltries fall . . . for we ship £15,000 in peltries which might have been pretty well sold here.[4]

⇒:⇐

WHILE MCTAVISH WAS successfully establishing himself in the fur business, others were doing the same. The genesis of the fur-trade company that would become known as the North West Company (NWC) dates back to 1775, when a large number of Montreal traders went to the Saskatchewan River country. They included the Frobisher brothers (Joseph and Thomas), the McGill brothers (James and John), Peter Pond, and Alexander Henry the Elder. Although he likely provided trade goods for Pond and others, McTavish never travelled beyond Grand Portage.

In June 1775, Henry left for the North West with sixteen canoes manned by fifty-two men, carrying goods and provisions to the value of three thousand pounds sterling. The other traders joined Henry along the way, and by the time they reached the Hudson's Bay Company (HBC) post at Cumberland House, the group numbered 30 canoes and 130 men. At Cumberland House, they separated into several groups. Henry and the Frobisher brothers decided to pool their stock and winter together, along with their forty employees. When the season was over, they divided the skins and meat they received in trade. Joseph Frobisher and Alexander Henry returned to Montreal, leaving Thomas Frobisher behind to continue trading. As Henry wrote, "This arrangement was beneficial to the merchants, but not directly so to the Indians . . . who paid greater prices than if a competition had subsisted."[5]

When Henry and Frobisher reached Lake of the Woods on their return trip, they met Natives who told them that "some strange nation had entered Montreal, taken Quebec, killed all the English, and would certainly be at the Grand Portage before we arrived there."[6] This was the first Henry and Frobisher had heard about the outbreak of the American Revolution. When they arrived back in Montreal in mid-October 1776, they discovered that the people at Lake of the Woods had slightly overstated the case, since the Americans had abandoned Montreal in May. Henry and Frobisher also learned that a group of prominent colonists had signed the Declaration of Independence on July 4, 1776. The Montreal merchants, although they had initially been against the Quebec Act, remained loyal to the British.

The first written reference to the NWC on record is in a letter written by an independent merchant named Lawrence Ermatinger in the fall of 1776. Ermatinger, who had ordered a large stock of trade goods from an English firm, asked this firm to use its influence in preventing a grant of exclusive trade to the NWC.[7]

John Askin, a merchant at Michilimackinac, had a long business relationship with the NWC. He wrote to Montreal merchants Isaac Todd and James McGill in June 1778 in this regard:

I assure you that tho' I now supply several others, besides the great Co. (as we must term them for distinction sake), I have certain inclination to forward their interest preferable to any other, and . . . no profit should induce me to undertake any thing that could in the least hurt a concern where so many of my friends are interested. "[8]

The explorer and fur trader Alexander Mackenzie described how the next steps were taken toward organizing the NWC. According to Mackenzie, in 1778 some of the traders in the Saskatchewan River country agreed to pool their excess goods, putting Peter Pond in charge of them. With four canoes, Pond proceeded to Athabasca country where he passed the winter of 1778–79. He procured twice as many furs of excellent quality as his canoes would carry, so he cached the excess furs and returned for them the following year.

The merchants were very excited when Pond arrived back east; however, they could not take advantage of his discoveries the following year because the governor of Quebec, General Frederick Haldimand, issued licences for canoes to go to the North West so late in the season that they could not possibly reach even the nearest wintering posts before freeze-up. When the merchants protested, Haldimand gave the excuse that the measure had been taken to prevent arms and ammunition from falling into rebel American hands. The following year, no licences at all were issued. The first formal NWC was organized in response to this situation; it was probably the first joint-stock company in North America. Even though this company lasted for only a single season, it convinced Governor Haldimand to issue licences in good time the following year.

During the winter of 1780, Charles Grant, a prosperous and respected Quebec merchant, visited Montreal in order to prepare a report on the state of the fur trade at the request of Governor Haldimand. Grant issued his report on April 24. He began by saying that he was making his report early so that Haldimand would be able to consider issuing passes for carrying on the current year's trade "as you may judge consistent with the welfare of commerce and the safety of the province." Grant wrote that furs had produced an annual return to Great Britain to the amount of £200,000 sterling in recent years. This amount, he continued, was "deserving of all the encouragement and protection which Government can with propriety give to that trade." If trade were under "great restraints or obstructed a few years, the consequences would prove ruinous" to the province, the traders, and the merchants of London. Stopping trade might also put the traders in danger as both their persons and property would probably "fall a sacrifice to the fury and rage of disappointed" Aboriginal residents.[9]

Governor Haldimand obviously was not convinced by the arguments of Grant and the fur traders, although he grudgingly issued more passes and allowed traders to carry more goods than he felt was wise. He commented:

> *The great demand for passes to the upper countries . . . at a time when the natural trade must necessarily diminish from the Indians being employed in war, created suspicions that means were found to convey supplies much wanted by the rebels into their country . . . I conceived the most effectual means to prevent the evil would be by permitting no more than a sufficient quantity of goods for the use of each post . . . in this, however, I have not been able to succeed.[10]*

John Askin was one of many people connected with the fur trade who were unhappy about shipping restrictions on the Great Lakes. On April 28, 1778, he wrote to Commodore Alexander Grant, McTavish's first employer and the man still in charge of naval vessels on the Great Lakes. Askin complained that he had a very considerable cargo in transit all of the previous year and that "no part of it arrived here which is a severe stroke to me." He begged Grant's assistance "in ordering it to be forwarded in the king's vessels." He went on to say that a single vessel could not carry "all the provisions necessary to support the trade of the country . . . [and] should the quantity fall short, even one-third, some of the people in the back country in all probability will perish for want. I thought it necessary to give you this information that you might acquaint the Governor with it, as it may not strike him in the same light."[11]

A few months later Governor Haldimand wrote to military leaders:

> *If the transport of any merchandise upon these lakes except in the king's vessels was permitted, a door would be opened for . . . illicit commerce which would be very hurtful to the trade of this province . . . we have had very recent instances of its being practiced over Lake Champlain by some of the most considerable merchants of Montreal, who are connected with great houses in London. It is attended by another great evil upon the Upper Lakes, that of introducing the Americans into the interior parts of the country, and giving them opportunities to debauch our friendly Indians and supplant us in the fur trade.*[12]

Constant protests by the merchants eventually brought relief. As a result of a petition dated October 4, 1784, Haldimand finally granted the NWC permission to build a thirty-four-foot boat to use on Lake Superior. Within a couple of years, the NWC had boats on all the Great Lakes except for Michigan.

After several short-term agreements, the NWC was radically reorganized in 1783. At that time, it was divided into sixteen shares held by nine men, including McTavish, the Frobisher brothers, Patrick Small, and Peter Pond. Management was entrusted to McTavish and the Frobishers, "for which they were to receive a stipulated commission in all transactions." Fittingly, the company adopted the motto "Perseverance" for their crest.

3 A NEW LAND, 1783—84

O fortress city, bathed by streams
Majestic as thy memories great,
Where mountains, floods, and forests mate.

. . .

Who hath not known delight whose feet
Have paced thy streets or terrace way;
From rampart sod or bastion grey
Hath marked thy sea-like river greet.

. . .

Then homeward, hearing song or tale,
With chimes of harness bells we sped
Above the frozen river bed
The city, through a misty veil,
Gleamed from her cape, where sunset fire
Touched louver and cathedral spire.
Bathed ice and snow a rosy red.

JOHN DOUGLAS SUTHERLAND CAMPBELL,
FROM "QUEBEC"

Little is known about the McGillivray family's activities over the six years between McTavish's visit to them in Scotland and William's arrival in Montreal in the summer of 1783. There is no record of where the McGillivray brothers attended school. Since William completed his education at the age of nineteen and then immediately began working as an apprentice clerk in his uncle's business, it seems likely that he received the equivalent of a high school education with some special training in accounting and other business subjects.

When William McGillivray arrived in Montreal, he had a few months to get to know the city before settling down to work when the fur brigades arrived in late summer. McTavish was too busy to spend much time with him during the day, so McGillivray likely spent much time walking around the city by himself. People told him that Montreal was second to Quebec City in size and wealth but first "on account of its fine situation and mild climate."[1] Montreal, which had been known as Ville Marie, had originally consisted of ten streets laid out in a rectangle and enclosed by a high stone wall. Three broad main streets ran parallel to the river; the other seven were perpendicular to these. By the time McGillivray arrived, Montreal had grown considerably and much of the original wall had been removed. Once a week, country people brought their produce for sale near the wharf on Rue Saint-Paul, and in late summer Rue de la Commune was transformed into the annual fur fair.

The city of Montreal, which had a population of less than nine thousand people in 1783, occupied only the south side of the island of Montreal. The lower level of Mont Royal, not yet part of Montreal, rose gently and was planted in gardens and orchards; the steeper upper slope was still wooded. Both the houses and warehouses of the principal merchants were spacious and covered with sheet iron or tin to protect them from fire. While most houses were built of timber, there also were a few stone mansions.

Houses commonly had benches on either side of the front door facing the street. There, families spent many fine summer evenings visiting with passersby. McGillivray found the young women attractive and very well dressed; however, he was likely too shy to do more than politely tip his hat to them. The young women, in their turn, undoubtedly took a great interest in McGillivray; an early painting shows him as a handsome, well-built young man with thick, curly red hair.

The arrival of the first canoes of the season at Lachine in late August was the most exciting event of the year for most Montreal residents. The fur-trade brigades had been gone since the ice went out of the rivers in late spring, and everyone anxiously awaited their return home. People could talk of nothing else. McGillivray found that he had to learn a whole new vocabulary in order to understand the conversations going on around him. Because he spoke French, he knew the literal meanings of most of the expressions he heard, but what he had to learn was what these expressions meant to Montrealers. For instance, les mangeurs de lard (pork eaters) were voyageurs who travelled only between Montreal and Grand Portage on Lake Superior. While their arrival back in Montreal was a cause for celebration, the return of les hommes du nord, or hivernants, was even more exciting. These men of the north, or winterers, would spend at least three years away from home, travelling beyond the Great Lakes to the North West. This was the country also known as le pays d'en haut, or high country. Les hommes du nord

At Lachine, near Montreal, voyageur canoes were unloaded before goods were transported to Montreal. This NWC warehouse at Lachine, built in 1803, is now part of the Fur Trade at Lachine National Historic Site of Canada. IRENE TERNIER GORDON

felt themselves much superior to the men who returned to their Quebec homes each winter.

Montreal dentist George Beers vividly described the return of les hommes du nord to Quebec:

The wild picturesque appearance of the men, and the distance they have come, awakens sympathy for them, and hundreds will go out from town to see them. Their appearance in the city is very odd. They go along the streets, gaping and staring at everything, in such haste and excitement that they run against people and stumble over little obstructions. They . . . look in the windows at the jumble of new things to them, and have a hearty laugh at what they consider the absurdities and curiosities of city people."[2]

Many people rushed to travel the nine miles of rough trail separating Montreal from Lachine so they would be first to greet the returning brigades. Lachine Falls prevented loaded canoes from travelling all the way to Montreal, so the goods had to be unloaded at Lachine and transferred to carts for transport to the Montreal warehouses. The quiet summer-time city that McGillivray was now accustomed to burst into life with the arrival of the brigades. The townspeople welcomed home husbands, fathers, sons, sweethearts, and friends. Church bells rang and flags waved. The voyageurs swarmed the narrow streets like schoolboys just let out of school—shouting and singing, greeting friends, telling tall tales, drinking too much, and recklessly spending money. Single men rekindled romances with the young women they had left behind or tried to impress new girls with tales of their derring-do. It is unlikely that McTavish, now a successful merchant, joined the throngs celebrating on the streets, but McGillivray almost certainly did.

McGillivray's first job once the brigades arrived was to tally the packs of furs as they arrived at the McTavish warehouse on the waterfront. The overpowering stench of untanned beaver pelts made him gag, and for the first few days he found it difficult to eat. After all the furs were tallied, McGillivray helped to repack them and transport them to the wharf for loading on ships bound for London. Finally, he helped his uncle pay off the voyageurs.

The city was relatively quiet for the few months between the departure of the ships for London with the year's take of furs and the beginning of the winter social season in December. Even when McTavish was at his busiest in summer, he led an active social life in the evenings. As a result, McGillivray had met most of his uncle's friends and business associates before the winter social season began. They included Alexander Henry, Joseph and Benjamin Frobisher, Charles Chaboillez, and James McGill.

Social life became livelier in December because travel was easier once the rivers froze over and there was enough snow on the ground for sleighs. Isaac Weld, a young man who visited Quebec about ten years after McGillivray first arrived, wrote:

Winter in Canada is the season of general amusement. The clear frosty weather no sooner commences than all thoughts about business are laid aside, and everyone devotes himself to pleasure. The inhabitants meet in convivial parties at each other's houses, and pass the day with music, dancing, card-playing and every social entertainment that can beguile the time . . . Such a constant and friendly intercourse is kept up amongst the inhabitants that I have often heard it mentioned that it appears then as if the town were inhabited but by one large family.[3]

The wealthier citizens travelled about in carioles in winter. These were light sleighs pulled by one or two horses that could carry two passengers and a driver. Although McGillivray was used to snow in winter, the temperature in the Highlands was above freezing more often than in Montreal. As a result, travel by cariole was speedier and more agreeable than winter travel in his homeland. All the men seemed to be in competition to have the handsomest outfit. Most carioles were open because the great pleasure of going for a cariole ride consisted in seeing others and being seen. The ladies always went out dressed in superb furs, and almost everyone looked as if they were enjoying themselves. Because carioles glided along so quietly, bells were attached to the horses' harnesses, and many drivers also had horns that they frequently sounded to guard against accidents.[4]

McGillivray may not have been aware of it, but not everyone in Montreal was enjoying winter parties in December 1783. On Christmas

Eve, some 550 men of the King's Royal Regiment of New York learned that their regiment had been disbanded since the British had lost the Revolutionary War. These men were not only unemployed but also had permanently lost their homes and lands in New York. They, along with their wives and children—a total of about 1,460 people—were crammed into a newly built barracks facing Jacques Cartier Square. To make matters worse, most of the women and children were infected with measles or smallpox. In addition, many other Loyalist refugees had sought safety in the city.

McTavish's friend James McGill was one of the two Montreal magistrates who asked the military commandant for assistance in keeping the peace. They feared riots and robberies in view of all the disbanded soldiers and Loyalist refugees wandering around the city. The commandant ordered a corporal and six soldiers to accompany a number of civilians in patrolling the street each night. They were ordered to "take up all soldiers found out of the barracks after hours and to apprehend any class of people who were suspected of being out on illegal purposes."[5] They only patrolled for a month but apparently put an end to any trouble.

City officials were also concerned with overcrowding in the city jail, which was described as being in "a ruinous condition, a nuisance to the public and dangerous to the health and lives of persons confined therein."[6] As a result, the city fathers organized a "gigantic" lottery in an attempt to raise enough money to construct a new jail. Unfortunately the news story does not indicate how successful the lottery was.

On Christmas Day 1783, the front page of the *Quebec Gazette* carried an address to the clergy of the city, imploring them to use their influence to persuade their congregations of the benefits of inoculation for smallpox. Another article stated that the magistrates had set the price of a four-pound loaf of white bread at 10½ pence. Brown bread was slightly cheaper, but still cost more than the refugees and the unemployed could comfortably pay. The same paper also carried an advertisement for ladies' tippets and muffs made of ground-squirrel fur, and gentlemen's caps and gloves lined with fur. All were described as very useful for winter travel.[7]

McGillivray may not have done much travelling outside of the immediate Montreal area during his first winter in North America, but undoubtedly he heard many stories of the perils of winter travel. Over the years to come, he might well have had an experience similar to the following, which took place on a trip between New York and Montreal. Because there was no public transportation between the two places, it was necessary for travellers to hire a driver with a team of horses and a sleigh. While crossing Lake Champlain, the narrator of this story was startled by "a swelling thunder-like noise, which sounded to me as passing from one end of the lake to the other." One of the hazards of crossing frozen bodies of water, which this traveller was not aware of, is suddenly encountering a pressure crack in seemingly safe ice. The horses pulling the traveller's sleigh were apparently accustomed to pressure cracks and able to stop safely; however, a sleigh and team immediately ahead of them could not stop in time and the horses tried to leap the wide crack. One horse made it safely and his harness was cut free from the sleigh, but the second horse fell into the water. The driver of the first sleigh took immediate action. He put the reins of one of his horses around the neck of the horse in the water "with a sliding knot which choked him." Then the men quickly passed the traces around that horse's body and "he floated like a bladder." The five men travelling in the two sleighs then succeeded in hauling the horse onto the ice. They rubbed him all over with straw until he was dry and "everyone contributed his great-coat to preserve some warmth." Shortly afterward, the "half-choked, half-drowned horse" rose to his feet. He was reharnessed, and in less than twenty minutes he was "in full vigour and spirits." At the same time, the driver of the sleigh that had not crossed the pressure crack, "taking a short run with his horses, cleared the crack in good style."[8]

Another acquaintance told McGillivray of an adventure he had while travelling in extremely cold weather. One night he opened a bottle of Madeira and found the wine frozen like snow except for a small quantity in the centre of the bottle. He poked a hole through to the liquid and drank it off. Since it was such a small drink, he did the same with a second bottle. Then he tried to walk down to the river but quickly found it so difficult to walk that he had to stagger back to the inn. Although he had only drunk the equivalent of one glass of Madeira, he later concluded—after finding the thawed wine tasted almost like water—that he had consumed the concentrated spirits of two bottles of wine on an empty stomach.[9]

There were at least short periods, both in fall and spring, when it was extremely dangerous or impossible to cross the St. Lawrence River. There were also longer periods when it was merely risky to cross; however, in an emergency there were always people willing to do so for payment or just because they enjoyed a challenge. McGillivray watched two such men take a traveller across the river one day in a canoe amid the most alarming confusion of ice islands "rushing along at a frightful speed." The men paddled from shore to the first ice island, landed on it, dragged the canoe across it, relaunched the canoe in open water, paddled to the next piece of ice and continued in this manner until they reached the opposite shore.[10]

The ice jammed up two or three times every winter before it was safe for the remainder of the season. One traveller had a frightening experience while staying in a second-floor room of a hotel facing the St. Lawrence in early December. The space between the hotel and the river filled with pieces of ice that formed "a confused wall of broken ice 20 feet higher than my window on the second floor," he reported. One huge sheet of ice looked as if "only the slightest puff of wind" would cause it to crash down to annihilate the hotel. The traveller was so alarmed that he rushed from his room and out onto the street. The hotel manager collected a large number of men with poles, ropes, and ladders to send the sheet of ice back into the river. Only then did the traveller consent to return to his room.[11]

Over the winter, McGillivray got to know Simon McTavish and his friends much better and learned a great deal from them about the fur trade. He listened to speculation about the Treaty of Paris (otherwise known as the Treaty of 1783) being drawn up at Versailles to end the American Revolutionary War. When a copy of the treaty finally arrived, the traders were angered by its terms. Quebec was to be greatly reduced in size, with the Americans receiving the territory of the Ohio and Mississippi Rivers and the posts of Detroit and Michilimackinac. McTavish and the Frobishers believed that the Southwest trade would be seriously disrupted; the McGill brothers thought the treaty would have a minimal effect on it. Over the course of the winter, the two groups agreed to split the fur-trade territory into two districts. The McGills and their associates would trade in the Southwest and the McTavish–Frobisher group would concentrate on the North West.

McGillivray also listened eagerly to the stories the veteran traders told about the history of the fur trade and their exploits as young men. Alexander Henry had particularly fascinating tales to tell and was a natural-born storyteller. He recounted how he came close to losing his life in the Rapides-des-Cèdres during the French and Indian War in 1760 while he was accompanying General Amherst and supplying provisions to his troops. Upward of one hundred soldiers were drowned in this accident. Henry was trapped in one of his boats on a rocky shelf in the middle of the rapids for hours until he was finally rescued by one of the general's aides-de-camp. Henry lost three boatloads of merchandise in the incident.

Even more exciting was Henry's account of how he survived the infamous baggataway massacre at Fort Michilimackinac on June 4, 1763. The Ojibwa had invited everyone at the fort to attend a game of baggataway (lacrosse) supposedly to celebrate the birthday of King George III. When Henry suggested to the fort commander that the Ojibwa might have a sinister motive for organizing the match, the commander "only smiled" at his suspicions. Henry decided to stay in his room and write letters while the game was on. Later in the afternoon, he heard a war cry followed by loud noises of general confusion. He rushed to his window and saw that a crowd of Ojibwa were inside the fort, cutting down and scalping all the Englishmen they encountered. He picked up his gun, expecting any moment to hear a drumbeat calling the soldiers to arms. When this did not happen, his only thought was to seek shelter. He could see that the Canadians were not being attacked, so he sneaked next door to the house of his Canadian neighbours and begged for shelter. Their slave woman hid Henry in the attic and locked the door.

When the slaughter was over, some men came to the neighbour's house and asked if he had any Englishmen in his house. The neighbour told them they could look for themselves. Henry had a few minutes in which to hide in a pile of birchbark sugar vessels while they found the key. He described what happened next:

The door was unlocked and . . . an instant after, four Indians entered the room, all armed with tomahawks, and all besmeared with blood . . . I could scarcely breathe; but I thought the throbbing of my heart occasioned a noise loud enough to betray me. The Indians walked in every direction about the garret, and one of them approached me so closely that . . . had he put forth his hand, he must have touched me. Still I remained undiscovered . . . [due to] the want of light in a room which had no window.[12]

Seventy soldiers stationed at the fort were killed. Henry was one of only twenty Englishmen who survived and were taken prisoner. Had he been discovered the day of the massacre instead of the following day, he likely would have been killed too. It is important to realize that at this time "Canadian" referred only to people of French origin. Those whose first language was English were called Englishmen, including Henry, who had been born in New Jersey.

McGillivray learned about the trading expedition made to the Saskatchewan River country by Henry and the Frobisher brothers in 1775 and also about how the NWC came into existence. He heard stories about the explorer and fur trader Samuel de Champlain, who first visited the Lachine Falls in 1603 and left an account of a double drowning there. Champlain had arranged to meet a large group of Huron and Algonquin for a fur-trading fair in the area. When they didn't turn up at the appointed time, Champlain sent two Native men and a French boy named Louis to look for them. Four days later, one of the men came back alone. He said that the other man had decided that they should shoot the rapids. The canoe struck a whirlpool and turned around many times before finally sinking. Only one of the men made it to shore. The lake and the falls were named in memory of Louis. Although the falls later became known as Lachine Falls, the lake is still known as Lac Saint-Louis. About the same time, the government set up fur fairs at Ville Marie (Montreal) and Trois Rivières to attract the Indians away from trading with the coureurs du bois.

All these tales of danger and high adventure would have fired the imagination of young William McGillivray during the long winter months. In the spring, his career in the fur trade would begin in earnest.

4 HEADING FOR LE PAYS D'EN HAUT, 1784

Sitting in my bark canoe
Swift as the arrow or the wind,
I defy any single force
The rapids of the St. Lawrence.

The farmer has his plow,
The hunter his gun, his dog,
The eagle has her nails and her sight.
Me, my boat, this is all I have.

FROM A TRANSLATION OF THE TRADITIONAL
VOYAGEUR SONG "MON CANOT D'ÉCORSE"

William McGillivray's first winter in Montreal finally came to an end. By mid-March, the temperature climbed to just above freezing most days, and the ice on the St. Lawrence slowly began to break up, although the river normally was not clear of ice for at least another month. The ice cracked from side to side with reports that sounded like cannon shots. Then, as the water rose due to the snow melt, the ice broke up and was forced rapidly downstream by wind and current. Ice jams were a constant concern, as pieces of ice were forced up against islands or piled into huge heaps in the river shallows. Sometimes these jams remained stationary, obstructing navigation for weeks; at other times they crashed into the shore, doing severe damage to wharves, riverfront buildings, trees, and fences.

Over the winter, McGillivray had signed a five-year contract with his uncle as an apprentice clerk at an annual salary of one hundred pounds. Like every apprentice, he received a basic kit of personal necessities, including clothing (corduroy pants and vest and four striped cotton shirts), bedding, a tent, hunting equipment, and a sort of picnic basket with dishes, kettle, and cutlery.

The date on which the brigades departed for Grand Portage varied from year to year, depending on when the ice went out of the river, usually in late April or early May. Great crowds of people gathered around the voyageurs for a week or two before they left.

Quebec historian Georges Dugas described the days leading up to the departure of the brigades:

> *During fifteen days, it was, for these old wolves of the North, a series of celebrations and amusements; they invited all their friends and revelled . . . The drink was flowing in torrents; in the evening they had a dance . . . On the day of departure, a crowd of people went to Lachine to witness the spectacle [and the voyageurs] embarked amidst the most enthusiastic cheers and firing of musketry.*[1]

McGillivray's first task as a new apprentice would have been to help load the trade goods and provisions into carts to be taken by road from Montreal to Lachine, where they would be transferred into the huge canots du maître (master's or Montreal canoes) in which they would travel between Lachine and Grand Portage. Loading the carts would have been a simple enough task for a strong young man like McGillivray; however, transferring the packs to the canoe would have been a different matter.

The canots du maître were about thirty-five to forty feet long and over six feet wide. Each carried sixty to sixty-five packs (pieces) of trade goods, each weighing about ninety pounds. In addition to the packs and a crew of ten or twelve men, the canoes also carried the men's baggage, provisions, and necessary tools and equipment. It was little wonder that voyageurs sometimes were not even allowed to carry a tent to sleep under, although they did carry oilcloth to keep the cargo dry. McGillivray would have been surprised to discover just how difficult it was to load a canoe properly. First, several long slender poles called grands-perches were placed across the bottom of the canoe to help evenly distribute the weight of the cargo and crew. Then, everything had to be placed precisely so that it took up the least amount of room possible and would not shift.

Lachine contained extensive warehouses, some belonging to the king and others to Montreal merchants. McGillivray was puzzled as to why the king would have warehouses in Lachine. McTavish explained that goods shipped from England, which would later be distributed as gifts to the Natives, were stored there before sending them upcountry. It was necessary for the commander of the Montreal garrison and a committee of merchants to inspect these goods and report to the government whether they met the terms of the contract and were of good value for the price paid for them.

Once the brigades left Lachine, they would make an important stop before they truly were underway. That stop was at the rapids at the village of Sainte-Anne, site of the church of Sainte-Anne-de-Bellevue, patron saint of the voyageurs. Most of the voyageurs went to confession there and attended Mass to pray for a safe and prosperous voyage. In the church, the voyageurs would each put a coin into a collection box. Although McGillivray was not a Catholic, he contributed his small coin like everyone else. Immediately after leaving the church, each man received a ration of rum. The next morning the canoes were reloaded and the voyage proper began.

Although McGillivray had learned much of the fur-trade vocabulary during his nine months in Montreal, he still had many more words to learn. Each brigade of between four and ten canoes was led by a bourgeois (an NWC partner) and a guide. The voyageurs were described by their positions in the canoes. Each canoe was manned by an avant (bow man) who kept watch on the river ahead and set the pace for paddling, a gouvernail or steersman in the stern, and five to ten milieux or middlemen. The voyageurs referred to the wind as la vieille, or old woman. If the wind and current were favourable they could put up a sail, thus temporarily increasing their speed while decreasing their paddling effort. In order to encourage la vieille to blow favourably, the voyageurs would throw pieces of tobacco into the water while chanting "Souffle, souffle, la vieille."

McGillivray travelled in McTavish's canoe, which proudly flew the new NWC flag. As he was the bourgeois, McTavish was carried on board his canoe on the back of one of the milieux so he would not get his feet wet. Then he comfortably seated himself on a mattress in the centre of the canoe. No doubt McGillivray initially was surprised to be accorded the same treatment. Since the ideal voyageur was a short, powerfully built man, the six-foot McGillivray likely found it embarrassing to be picked up like a child by someone six or eight inches shorter than he was, but he quickly learned that height was not an advantage when travelling in a heavily loaded canoe. Should McGillivray have argued against this special treatment, McTavish would have responded that he had no choice but to follow established procedures. People in the fur trade, McGillivray was told, revealed their social status both by their behaviour and by their dress. "Men of dignity must deck themselves better than the common voyageur if they wish to be considered as they should be . . . There must be some thing in the outward appearance to attract notice and command respect."[2]

One of the last things the brigade had done before leaving Lachine was to send a couple of men to a neighbouring Aboriginal village to purchase a supply of birchbark, pine gum, and wattap (split spruce roots) for repairing the canoes. These were crucial items to every brigade. Although birchbark canoes could carry surprisingly heavy loads, despite their fragile appearance, they were also easily damaged and required frequent repairs. Within the first two weeks of their trip, McGillivray's brigade had to make repairs at least three times. One canoe suffered three broken ribs, and the next day another suffered a broken bow when it ran against the shore. Acquiring sufficient canoes and keeping them in good repair was an ongoing concern for fur traders.

McGillivray soon learned the different ways of moving a canoe through sections of a river where it was dangerous or otherwise impossible to paddle. Tracking, or lining, was a way of going upstream if the current was too strong to paddle against. Men wore shoulder harnesses with lines attached to the canoe and walked along the shore, towing the canoe like canal horses. One modern canoeist describes the procedure as being like walking a dog on a short leash. Only the steersman stayed on board the canoe. If it was impossible to walk along the riverbank, the men poled the canoe if the water was shallow and the river bottom sufficiently firm. The men who did the poling had to have excellent balance as they stood in the canoe and pushed it along with eight- or ten-foot metal-tipped poles called perches.

Anything was easier than portaging, which was the last resort. The men each carried two pièces at a time over the portage. One was placed in a sling or tumpline which went over a man's forehead and rested in the small of his back. A second pièce rested above the first in the hollow behind his neck. A man travelled the portage at a shuffling trot with his back slightly bent. Unless the portage was very short, the men would stop for about ten minutes every half hour at what was called a pose. There they would drop their load and go back for a second load to give themselves a rest. A mile-long portage would require walking at least five miles and would take several hours.

Like most young men, McGillivray was unlikely to have been overly concerned about danger; however, he hadn't been underway for many days before he realized just how risky canoe travel could be. He noticed that the voyageurs had a custom of taking off their hats and making the sign of the cross whenever they passed a place where someone had died accidentally and been buried. Because there were crosses at almost every rapid they encountered, the men said their prayers much more frequently than they did at home. At one place McGillivray counted thirty crosses.

When they reached a set of rapids called Décharge Dufort, named after a man who drowned there, McGillivray learned the difference between a portage and a décharge. Both canoes and cargo had to be carried over a portage. At a décharge, on the other hand, the canoes were taken down the rapids empty and the voyageurs carried only the cargo. On June 7, they reached Grand Calumet, which was the longest portage on the Ottawa River. It took more than twenty-four hours to complete, including time spent mending canoes.

A terrible accident took place on Lake Nipissing shortly after McGillivray's brigade passed by there. Eleven men perished, along with their canoes and cargo, although the men with his brigade would not learn about it until the following year. To mark the site, a high bluff on the southeast shore of the lake was named Pointe aux Croix and eleven crosses were erected there.

Danger aside, the daily routine of the voyageur was gruelling. The day began at dawn—sometime between 2 and 4 AM—when the voyageurs

Voyageurs run the rapids on central Ontario's Mattawa River in this engraving from a painting by Frances Anne Hopkins. PROVINCIAL ARCHIVES OF MANITOBA/HBC ARCHIVES N16859

were roused with shouts of "C'est l'heure à se lever" (time to get up). This was usually contracted to "St'r lever! St'r lever!" or something less polite.

The men left at daylight without breakfast. Finally, shortly before 8 AM, they stopped to eat. Lunch may have been a piece of pemmican eaten while paddling or portaging. Every hour they stopped long enough to smoke their pipes. This break was so important that distances came to be measured in pipes. A distance of trois (three) pipes might be fifteen to twenty miles depending on wind and current. At nightfall, between 8 and 10 PM, they made camp and had a hot meal.

If a portage was necessary, the canoe was brought close to shore but left in deep enough water to prevent damage from rocks. The avant then jumped into the water and steadied the canoe for the gouvernail who followed him. These two held the canoe while the milieux got out. Then, any passengers were carried to shore by the milieux before the freight was unloaded. The avant and gouvernail carried the canoe, while the milieux carried the freight. Voyageurs often worked between fifteen and eighteen hours a day. The number and duration of rest stops depended on how rushed the brigade was. Poor weather and damage to the canoes could cause delays.

Each voyageur had his own paddle, which was like a lucky charm and an extension of his own arm. Some were brightly painted. They might have been handed down from the voyageur's father and been blessed by the local priest. The favourite wood for paddles was basswood—stronger than spruce or pine and lighter than birch or maple. In addition to his paddle, each man carried a drinking cup tied to his sash. These cups were carved from hardwood burls and decorated with a wide variety of incised motifs, including the name of the owner. One man had a cup shaped like a turtle shell; its handle was a naked man (Atlas) holding up the earth. Other cups had handles representing various animals.

After more than a month of unremitting labour, the brigade finally reached Lake Superior. Just before arriving at Grand Portage at the far end of the lake, they paused long enough for the men to shave and don their best clothes. McTavish put on his fine beaver hat, which he carried in a special hat box. When they were within sight of Grand Portage, the voyageurs paddled madly up to the shore "as if they meant to dash the canoe to splinters," singing lustily all the while.[3] Just when McGillivray thought they could not possibly avoid hitting the shore, the men back-paddled. The avant then sprang onshore and stopped the canoe dead by seizing the bow. The whole population of Grand Portage rushed to greet the canoes, some firing guns in honour of the bourgeois. Everyone shook hands, and all were greeted as brothers, except for the bourgeois, who was addressed as if he were their father.

While at Grand Portage, the guides and interpreters had indoor sleeping accommodations and messed in the Great Hall along with les hommes du nord. They were regaled with bread and butter, meat, fish, potatoes, tea, wine, spirits, and plenty of milk and tobacco. The voyageurs were lodged in tents outside of the fort and ate mainly corn, just as they had while underway. The men from each interior post had their own campsites. To minimize clashes between the two groups, their camps were separated from those of les mangeurs du lard by a brook.

There is no record of what work McGillivray did at Grand Portage on his first visit there. He possibly clerked in the equipment shop, checked furs as the wintering partners brought them in, or transferred goods from les canots du maître to les canots du nord. All goods brought from

Montreal had to be transferred to smaller canoes to be carried to les pays d'en haut because the rivers beyond Grand Portage were not deep enough for les canots du maître. The smaller north canoes were about twenty-five feet long with a crew of four to six men and were capable of carrying about 3,500 pounds of cargo and crew.

Although the men still had to work to do, the annual Grand Portage rendezvous was also a time of celebration. The voyageurs could purchase food, drink, and other goods. Many made their purchases on credit and ended up owing more money than they had earned. The partners and clerks had their own store with more costly goods for sale. When the bourgeois' business meetings were over and the goods all organized, the rendezvous ended with a banquet for the gentlemen, followed by a ball in the dining room with bagpipes, violin, flute, and fife. The countrywomen were dressed in their finest clothes and "danced not amiss" at the ball.[4] The local Ojibwa also had a dance in the fort, and the NWC gave them thirty-six gallons of shrub, a punch made of sweetened fruit juice and rum.

McGillivray had quickly learned that voyageurs loved to talk and boast about their prowess. At Grand Portage, he met a number of older voyageurs who entertained him with highly suspect versions of their life stories. They boasted of saving the lives of bourgeois and of the large numbers of wives, horses, and dog teams they had. One particularly voluble individual stated that "No portage was too long for me . . . [and] fifty songs a day were nothing to me. I could carry, paddle, walk and sing with any man I ever saw."[5] According to him, no bourgeois had better-dressed wives, no chief had finer horses, and no man had better-harnessed or swifter dogs than he did. With time and experience, McGillivray would come to realize that not only did voyageurs love to talk and show off their physical prowess, but they also had a practical reason for doing so. They hoped to impress their bourgeois and thus negotiate better working conditions or wages from them.

After the ball, McGillivray departed for the North West with the wintering partners and les hommes du nord, travelling in a brigade of five canots du nord while his uncle returned to Montreal. Although McGillivray had learned a lot over the months since he left Montreal, during the upcoming fall and winter, he would no longer have his uncle beside him for advice and support.

5 "JE SUIS UN HOMME DU NORD," 1784—94

What would Susan say?
Would she say that she was happy
To be given by her father
To the blue-eyed stranger from so far away?
What would Susan say?

Were you married at the river
From his post of Île-à-la-Crosse,
Forest girl from the North Saskatchewan?
What would Susan say?

RODNEY BROWN
FROM "WHAT WOULD SUSAN SAY?"[1]

In mid-August, the brigade reached the height of land west of Grand Portage where the rivers began their descent to Hudson Bay. Here, William McGillivray experienced the ceremony that every first-time traveller to le pays d'en haut was required to undergo upon reaching this landmark. The head guide cut a cedar bough and dipped it in water. He then commanded McGillivray to kneel and "baptized" him by sprinkling water on his head. "Now," the guide told him, "you must swear to follow the code of the voyageurs—never allow any other novice to pass this way without taking the oath and never kiss another voyageur's wife without her permission. Then you will be able to call yourself un homme du nord." McTavish had warned McGillivray that he would be expected to stand drinks for the whole brigade as part of the ceremony. The ceremony ended with a dozen gunshots fired off as the men enjoyed their drinks.

By the end of August, the brigade finally arrived at the south end of Lake Winnipeg, where the Red River flows into the lake. Soon after, they reached the junction of the Red and Assiniboine Rivers, commonly known as The Forks, site of the modern city of Winnipeg. Here they headed onto the Assiniboine River. McGillivray was impressed with his first sight of the plains along the river, and within a few days he was excited to see his first buffalo. His reaction was no doubt similar to that of fur trader John MacDonnell, who joined the NWC about a decade after McGillivray and wrote in his diary, "We have walked on delightful plains . . . The river winds so that we can keep ahead of the canoes and have enough time to hunt and fish." Hunting and fishing would have been pleasant diversions after long weeks of sitting in a canoe; more importantly, they provided a welcome change of diet, as brigades normally had to travel so quickly that they carried all their food with them. MacDonnell also commented that by the time they reached the end of their trip, "The remains of the biscuit we brought from the Grand Portage has been so bruised in the carrying places that we find it now most convenient to eat it with a spoon."[2]

McGillivray spent his first winter in le pays d'en haut working under bourgeois Robert Grant. He snowshoed from camp to camp, bargaining with Sioux and Plains Cree for pemmican and furs. The Assiniboine country was more important for pemmican than for pelts. The following spring, Grant and McGillivray were the first winterers back at Grand Portage, where they met Roderick McKenzie, a clerk for a Montreal trading company that was in competition with the NWC. McKenzie wrote of their meeting, "These gentlemen were of the opposition and strangers to me—but I called upon them and was well pleased with my reception"[3]

In the summer of 1785, McGillivray went to Île-à-la-Crosse on the upper Churchill River with bourgeois Patrick Small. As well as being a partner of McTavish, Small was considered one of the ablest NWC traders and it is likely that McTavish assigned his nephew to apprentice under Small for that reason. Small sent McGillivray to found a new outpost on Lac des Serpents, several days' journey from Île-à-la-Crosse. When he arrived, he found Roderick McKenzie already there. Small had ordered McGillivray to build his post alongside McKenzie's, but McGillivray did not approve of the building site McKenzie had selected. "I was told of a much better site nearby in the vicinity of a small river that is supposed to be full of fish," he told McKenzie, who agreed that they should both go there.[4]

When bourgeois Alexander Mackenzie, who was on his way to Athabasca country, left his cousin Roderick McKenzie at Lac des Serpents, he told him to watch out for McGillivray's interpreter, a man named Cartier, whom he described as "a very keen insinuating fellow." Alexander instructed Roderick to "keep everything as secret as you can from your men; otherwise these old voyageurs will fish all they know out of your green hands." Cartier, who had one of the longest fur-trade careers on record, appears prominently in McGillivray's Île-à-la-Crosse journal of 1793. According to the HBC Northern Department servant's accounts in 1824, Cartier, who was then aged seventy-two, had a fifty-seven-year career in the fur trade.[5]

The NWC had a much larger operation in le pays d'en haut than did Gregory McLeod, the company employing the Mackenzie cousins. The NWC sent twenty-five canoes of trade goods from Grand Portage, but Gregory McLeod sent only nine. The NWC had 250 men, Gregory McLeod only 90. As a beginning trader at Lac des Serpents, McGillivray likely only had as many goods as would fit in a single north canoe, which also had to carry four or five men and their personal effects.

McGillivray and Roderick McKenzie were almost the same age and had a similar Highland background. They became close friends over the course of a winter spent "within gunshot of one another." In the spring, they travelled together with their men back to Île-à-la-Crosse. "Our canoes arrived side by side, the crews singing in concert. Notwithstanding the surprise the chorus caused, we were both well received at the waterside by our respective employers. McGillivray and I lived on friendly terms ever after," McKenzie wrote.[6]

McGillivray was supposed to spend the summer trading for pemmican; however, when he arrived at Île-à-la-Crosse, Small wanted to leave for Grand Portage immediately so asked him to remain there until trader Peter Pond arrived from Lake Athabasca. Roderick also stayed at Île-à-la-Crosse, awaiting the arrival of Alexander Mackenzie's partner, John Ross. The two young clerks were shocked when Pond finally arrived and reported that Ross had been killed, allegedly in a scuffle at Athabasca with some of Pond's men over fishing nets. Although the employees of the two companies disagreed on many points about how Ross had died, this was the second time in Pond's fur-trade career that he had been involved with a murder. In spite of Small's written orders that McGillivray spend the summer procuring pemmican, he decided to go to Grand Portage to inform his uncle, who would be there for the annual rendezvous, of Ross's death and Pond's connection to it. McKenzie decided to go to Grand Portage for the same reason. The two men delegated their pemmican duties to other clerks and set off with the best available paddlers, arriving at Grand Portage before the partners of either the NWC or Gregory McLeod had completed their annual meetings.

As a result of the violence, McTavish proposed that the NWC and Gregory McLeod should join together. The Gregory McLeod partners —John Gregory, Norman McLeod, Peter Pangman, and Alexander Mackenzie—agreed.

McGillivray spent the next winter at Île-à-la-Crosse, while the Mackenzie cousins both went to Lake Athabasca. Despite the distance separating them, the three men managed to meet at least once over the winter. They "walked their six or seven hundred miles on snow shoes for the pleasure of taking a Christmas dinner with a friend."[7] In the spring, they travelled from Île-à-la-Crosse to Grand Portage together.

At the 1789 rendezvous, McGillivray was posted north of the lower Saskatchewan River, near present-day Flin Flon, Manitoba. The Rat River (Les Rats, as the voyageurs called it) was a promotion for McGillivray because competition would be much keener due to the long presence of the HBC in the area. The HBC post at Cumberland House was only a two-day journey from McGillivray's post. Unfortunately, only fragments of the journal he kept in 1789–90 still exist. McGillivray noted of Rat River, "Our intelligence as to the number of Indians in that quarter has always been false. We were made to believe by . . . all that pretended to know the country that there were 50 to 60 Indians, instead of which there are only 10 men belonging to the place."[8]

McGillivray had become an aggressive trader. He intercepted many people who traditionally traded with the HBC. Of one such band, he wrote that if they went back to HBC it would be "because I cannot prevent them, as I shall use promises and menaces (if goods fail) to deter them from their purpose." On the other hand, when a trapper reminded him that he could trade with the HBC, McGillivray responded sharply. "I told him that they knew the way and that they were at liberty. That their loss would not give me any pain as they were so troublesome."[9]

McGillivray was also persistent in going after unpaid debts. "I was no welcome guest among them, but seeing my determination to have my credits, they were very quiet; if they had been otherwise they would have broken my neck." In another instance, he wrote of a family from a rich trading area who had arrived with scarcely enough pelts to pay their debts and none to carry them over the summer, "I gave them a hearty set down for their laziness—told them that I had much rather they remained all upon their lands than come now to the fort so poor to make me and themselves ashamed."[10]

Despite his forceful approach to business, McGillivray claimed that during his nine years as a winterer he "never confined or punished a servant for ill conduct."[11] On the other hand, when voyageurs at Lac la Pluie went on strike for higher wages in 1794, his brother Duncan, who had arrived in North America after William, sent the strike's leaders to Montreal in chains. According to Duncan, "A few discontented persons in their band, wishing to do as much mischief as possible assembled their companions together several times on the voyage outward and represented to them how much their interest suffered by the passive obedience to the will of their masters." On arrival at Lac la Pluie, the crew threatened to return to Montreal without the cargo if they did not receive higher wages. The bourgeois quickly managed to prevail upon a few of the men to abandon the strike. Soon afterward, most of the others returned to work.[12]

At the end of his first season at Les Rats, McGillivray had seventy-eight packs of furs and six bags of castoreum. The final entry in his journal listed the leftover goods he was leaving behind for the trader who would replace him, followed by the words, "the end of William McGillivray at Rivière Meline, 13th June, 1790. *Adieu Les Rats*."[13] On his way to Grand Portage, McGillivray headed for Grand Rapids, a popular meeting place for fur traders, where the Saskatchewan River flowed into Lake Winnipeg.

When the brigades reached Grand Rapids in 1790, they celebrated Alexander Mackenzie's explorations to the Arctic with "eggnog" made with "sturgeon roe stirred smartly while pouring in the rum."[14]

As a clerk, McGillivray was not entitled to attend the business meetings held at the Grand Portage summer rendezvous, but he would have looked forward to seeing friends there and especially to reunions with his uncle. At the 1790 rendezvous, he received some very welcome news. Peter Pond had retired, and McGillivray was the clerk nominated to purchase Pond's NWC share for eight hundred pounds. This made him a wintering partner at the age of twenty-six. He was given responsibility for the English (Churchill) River department, with headquarters at Île-à-la-Crosse, where about eighty men and forty women lived. The following year, when Alexander Mackenzie went on furlough and Patrick Small retired, McGillivray was also given charge of the Athabasca department, thus becoming the bourgeois in charge of a huge area stretching from the Saskatchewan River to the Rockies.

One of the major duties of a bourgeois was to trade for pemmican, the most important item of the fur traders' diet. McGillivray occasionally enjoyed a buffalo hunt. One of the main sites for the hunt and manufacture of pemmican was Fort des Prairies on the North Saskatchewan River, where the NWC even maintained some special buffalo-hunter horses. Another was Lac d'Orignal Post, established in 1789 by Angus Shaw on the Beaver River northeast of Edmonton. Shaw would later marry McGillivray's sister Margery.

Little is known about McGillivray's personal life while in the North West. About 1789 or 1790, he married a Cree or Métis woman called Susan, who was born near Flin Flon on the Manitoba–Saskatchewan border. William and Susan had four children. The eldest was a daughter named Elizabeth. On March 1, 1791, Susan gave birth to twin sons, Simon and Joseph, named for Simon McTavish and Joseph Frobisher. They were baptized on October 3, 1796, in Montreal with Joseph Frobisher and Alexander Mackenzie standing as their godfathers. A third son, Peter, named after Peter Pond, died at a very young age.

There is no evidence that McGillivray lived with Susan after 1793, but since he never returned to the North West after that year, she must have gone to Grand Portage before 1796, when the twins were taken to Montreal to be baptized. There is also a record of payment to Susan and

Elizabeth for making sashes at Fort William, but unfortunately there is no date on that document.[15]

In June 1793, McGillivray left the west for the last time. He reported eighteen canoes of goods from all the posts on the English River. This included 392 packs of furs and 34 kegs of castoreum. About one hundred packs were left inland. The last entry in his journal was dated June 14, when he arrived at The Pas and met Angus Shaw, with whom he travelled to Grand Portage.

⧨

WHILE TRAVEL TO and from the North West was gruelling and often dangerous, there was occasionally some relief from the hardship. The men on the brigades' return trips from Grand Portage looked forward to reaching Lake Winnipeg. If the wind was favourable there, they could lash their canoes together and hoist sails. Then, instead of the backbreaking work of paddling, the voyageurs could drift north, smoking their pipes and sharing tales. Alternatively, brigades from various posts might challenge each other to canoe races. These races inevitably favoured the Lake Athabasca brigades, which were handpicked teams using smaller canoes and carrying lighter loads. Instead of delivering their furs to Grand Portage or Fort William, they only went as far as Fort Lac la Pluie, an advance depot built so that brigades would be able to make the return trip to Athabasca country before freeze-up. The Athabasca crews would start the contest by taunting slower canoes. Bets were laid and the race was on. Some paddlers reached a rate of fifty-five or sixty strokes per minute, compared to the normal forty-five strokes per minute.

One marathon race in 1794 lasted for 48 hours, only halting at the order of Duncan McGillivray, who described what happened:

> *On the second night of the contest one of our steersmen being* ·
> *overpowered by sleep fell out of the stern of his canoe, which being*
> *under sail advanced a considerable distance before the people*
> *could recover from the confusion that this accident occasioned . . .*
> *[T]he poor fellow . . . cried out to two canoes that happened to*
> *pass within a few yards of him to save his life pour l'amour de*
> *dieu, but neither the love of God or of the Blessed Virgin . . . had*

the least influence on his hard hearted countrymen . . . He must
certainly have perished if his own canoe had not returned.[16]

The brigades celebrated their return to their posts after the summer rendezvous with homecoming balls. The bourgeois and his wife led the first dance, followed by the second-in-command and his wife. Only then did everyone else get up on the floor. When McGillivray first arrived at Île-à-la-Crosse, Small and his wife opened the dance, followed by McGillivray and Susan. At one such ball, seventy-two men, thirty-seven women, and sixty-five children were in attendance in a twenty-two- by twenty-three-foot room where the adults danced until daybreak.

⇒:⇐

IT IS NOT known exactly when William McGillivray's brother Duncan arrived in North America. William had come to Montreal soon after finishing school at the age of nineteen. If Duncan did the same, he could have arrived as early as 1787. After the 1794 rendezvous, William accompanied Duncan on the first day of his trip to Fort George, an NWC post on the North Saskatchewan River. On August 24, Duncan noted in his journal that they arrived at Bourbon (Cedar) Lake where "we found my brother's relations, with whom we traded some provisions and paid them some credits [due] since last spring."[17] No mention is made of Susan, but she quite possibly was part of the group.

When Duncan arrived at Cumberland House at the end of August, he found everyone excited about an attack on the HBC's South Branch House by the Gros Ventre.[18] HBC factor William Tomison, who was on his way to his company post of Buckingham House near Fort George, had been waiting at Cumberland House for ten days for the Nor'Westers to arrive so that the two groups could travel together. Duncan wrote that everyone was so nervous that scarcely a day passed "without producing appearances which are supposed to portend immediate danger . . . A buffalo, a stag & a wolf have been successively mistaken for Gros Ventre." The traders only began to relax somewhat after they met some Assiniboine near the Battle River who told them that the Gros Ventre had escaped to the Rocky Mountains immediately after their attack on South Branch.[19]

Duncan described Fort George as a place of "extensive trade . . . surrounded by numerous tribes of Indians." When a band approached the fort, the chief usually sent several young men ahead to announce their arrival and to receive the few gifts that they normally were given on these occasions: some powder, a piece of tobacco, and a little paint for their faces. When almost at the gate, the men would salute the traders by firing off their guns. The traders responded by hoisting a flag and firing a few shots. Only then would the chiefs or other leading men enter the fort, where they were disarmed and treated to a few drams and a bit of tobacco. After smoking for some time, they related the news "with great deliberation and ceremony relaxing from their usual taciturnity in proportion to the quantity of rum they have swallowed."

During this time, the women had set up camp outside the fort. Duncan notes that the adults were given free drinks of rum for twenty-four hours or more before the actual trading began—the amount of drinks in proportion "to the nation and to the quality of the chiefs." Les gens du large (wandering tribes) of the plains were "treated with less liberality" than were the Woodland Cree and Ojibwa trappers because the commodities of les gens (chiefly horses, wolves, fat, and pemmican) were less in demand than were beaver pelts.[20]

The use of alcohol in trade caused many problems. It is not known what William's attitude was toward this issue; however, Duncan commented on it extensively in his journal:

> *In these debauches [as a result of giving generous amounts of rum]*
> *we take every precaution to prevent bloodshed . . . for a quarrel*
> *betwixt any two tribes may occasion revolutions which would*
> *be very prejudicial to the concern; besides we are commanded by*
> *humanity to preserve the lives of our fellow creatures where it is in*
> *our power, and to protect the oppressed . . . This kind of assistance is*
> *often necessary in Indian country, where the weak become naturally*
> *a prey to the strong, and where force is universally supposed to*
> *confer right . . . Since our arrival this has been one continued scene*
> *of drunkenness and riot, of clamour and confusion.*[21]

On November 25, the Blackfoot arrived near Fort George. In order to secure a friendly reception, they sent several Cree chiefs to the fort with offers to return all the horses the Blackfoot had stolen from the Nor'Westers the previous year. Early in the morning of November 26, a group of twelve young men came to get tobacco for twenty Blackfoot and Blood chiefs. Shortly afterward, the whole band appeared on the river. About thirty of the men headed to the HBC fort, while seventy or eighty others marched slowly to the NWC fort. At the gate, fourteen chiefs leading fourteen horses advanced and delivered the horses to Shaw, the bourgeois in charge of Fort George. The men left their arms with the women, likely because they feared placing them in the hands of the traders, as was the custom. Shaw was not satisfied with the number of horses the Blackfoot brought and sent some of his men, including Duncan, to choose ten more horses from their camp.

Duncan, who was noted for his hot temper, was enraged to learn that the individuals who had robbed him of his horses the previous year were not present. As a result, he entered the hall where the principal men were assembled and, in his words, "sprung upon their greatest chief Gros Blanc and offered him an indignity which he will always remember with anger and resentment." Gros Blanc, who was feared by all his neighbours due to his immense size and his personal courage, had the reputation of being "the most daring and intrepid Indian" in the whole area.[22]

As a result of his attack on Gros Blanc, Duncan received a horse and some finely ornamented robes and clothing. Gros Blanc threatened violence against Duncan, but his relations persuaded him against it. The next day, "a general peace was concluded betwixt all parties." In Duncan's opinion, his actions had a good effect on the behaviour of the Blackfoot:

From being insolent and overbearing they are become entirely submissive and comport themselves with great circumspection to avoid giving offence. They even deliver up their women to the unlawful embraces of the men to purchase their lost favour—a custom hitherto held in some kind of dishonour among the tribe. The men also no longer bargained so hard and accepted much worse deals than previously.[23]

Duncan realized that the plains provided such a rich living that the Natives could live very happily without the assistance of trade goods. Thus it is "our luxuries that attract them to the Fort and make us so necessary to their happiness." Rum and tobacco were the greatest luxuries, while ammunition "is rendered valuable by the great advantage it gives them over their enemies."[24] Blackfoot chief Gros Blanc did not return to the fort the next spring but sent a long message to Shaw saying that Duncan had offered him an insult that "no man breathing ever did before." As a mark of his forgiveness, however, he wanted to adopt Duncan as his little brother to replace his brother who had been killed the previous summer in a war with the Snakes.[25]

Although William never returned to the North West after 1793, Duncan spent much of the remainder of his life there. The brothers were close, despite their very different characters, and were both ambitious men who were anxious to further their fur-trade careers. While William was delighted to leave the North West and carry on his work from Montreal, Duncan was an avid explorer who believed that the NWC needed to expand beyond the Rocky Mountains.

6 MONTREAL: BUILDING THE NORTH WEST COMPANY, 1784–94

Knights of the roundtable, let us drink to see if the wine is good.
I would drink five or six bottles with a woman on my knee.
If the wine is good, if it is agreeable, I would drink to my pleasure.
If I die, I want to be interred in a cave where there is good wine.
My two feet against the wall and my head under the spigot.
And if the cask flows, I would drink at my leisure.
On my tomb I wish one would write,
"Here lies the king of the drinkers."

(Chorus)

J'en borai cinq à six bouteilles,
Une femme sur mes genous.
J'en borai cinq à six bouteilles,
Une femme, oui, oui, oui
Une femme, non, non, non
Une femme sur mes genoux.

FROM "CHEVALIERS DE LA TABLE RONDE,"
A TRADITIONAL VOYAGEUR SONG

hile William McGillivray was travelling and working in the North West, his uncle, Simon McTavish, had continued to build and strengthen the NWC. McTavish and the Frobisher brothers had been friends and business colleagues since at least 1775. After Benjamin Frobisher had died in April 1787,[1] McTavish wrote to Joseph suggesting that they join forces because Benjamin's death would "encourage those who wish to support Gregory." This was just before McGillivray and Roderick McKenzie learned of the murder of John Ross in Athabasca country, which would result in the union of Gregory McLeod and the NWC later that summer. McTavish suggested the following plan as the best solution for both him and Frobisher:

> I should be at a loss to attend the outfits and other business here, and go every year to the Portage . . . We at present hold between us near one-half of the concern . . . and I see no means so likely to support our consequence in that country as to join our fortunes and names in a general co-partnership, one-half to each . . . It will be prudent to confine ourselves entirely to trade in the North West, which we can attend to well enough by one of us going up every summer."[2]

The Frobisher brothers had been in business together since they arrived in Montreal from England in the 1760s. Benjamin, who had the best talent for organization and administration, became company manager, while Joseph served as a first-rate deputy. The third brother, Thomas, spent almost his entire career trading in the North West. Immediately following Benjamin's death, Joseph had assured their London suppliers that the business would not suffer by his brother's death because "I am thoroughly acquainted with every branch of it."[3]

A week later, however, Joseph admitted to McTavish that he had "never, as you know, taken any part in the management of the general concern of our house here," and he agreed that "throwing our interests together seems to be the most certain means of giving stability to our concern and defeating the hopes which our opponents may form from the distressing event of my poor brother's death."[4]

Once it was organized, McTavish, Frobisher & Co. became solely responsible for financing, importing trade goods, hiring men, and selling pelts for the NWC. The following year, one of their two London suppliers informed the company that they would no longer be supplying goods for them. As a direct result of this problem McTavish decided to form his own house, McTavish, Fraser & Co., in London in 1788. He entrusted management of the new company to his cousin John Fraser, a businessman thoroughly knowledgeable about trading on both sides of the Atlantic. The new company minimized the uncertainties of selling pelts, purchasing goods, and obtaining credit and insurance.

Within a few years, McTavish was firmly in command of McTavish, Frobisher & Co. Although Joseph Frobisher did very well financially, he was unhappy with his role within the new McTavish, Frobisher & Co. Despite his admission that he had never taken an active role in the management of the House of Frobisher, he still considered himself "the principal of the [new] house." In 1791, he pointed out that his role was now limited "to outdoor business, hiring of men and public duty."[5] Since this apparently was what he had done before Benjamin's death, he should not have been dissatisfied. Relations between Frobisher and the other partners became more difficult as McTavish spent increasing amounts of time in London. In November 1794, James Hallowell wrote regarding Frobisher, "I am sorry that any expression of mine should seem intended to amend his feeling. We are convinced of his abilities, and have the fullest confidence in his honour, although we have in some instances differed in opinion."[6]

By the agreement of 1787, the NWC was divided into twenty shares. McTavish, Frobisher & Co. held seven of these (three belonging to Frobisher and four to McTavish). As well, four other shares were virtually controlled by them. A new agreement was negotiated in 1790 whereby McTavish, Frobisher & Co. became the sole agents of the NWC in Montreal. About this time, John Gregory and James Hallowell also became partners in McTavish, Frobisher & Co.

In the fall of 1791, new competitors emerged against the NWC, including the two firms of Todd, McGill & Co. and Forsyth, Richardson & Co. The latter company included Alexander Henry the Elder. Several months later, Frobisher wrote to McTavish, who was in London, saying that McGill suggested that the NWC might increase the number of their shares to twenty-four and give the extra four shares to their rivals "on condition that the house of McTavish, Frobisher & Co. should have the management of the whole business both in London and Montreal." Frobisher also told McGill that if he and his associates would wait until the fall of 1792, "when the feelings of both sides would have become clearer, something might be arranged."[7]

In London, John Fraser agreed with Frobisher. McTavish evidently did not, because Fraser warned him in May 1792 against "losing the ladle full for the lickings." Fraser suggested that making a small sacrifice now was preferable to the certain expense of repelling later attacks "and the risk of being obliged in the end to give double what would satisfy now."[8] The matter was resolved in September, at least temporarily, when the number of shares in the NWC was increased to forty-six.

Merchant John Askin continued to deal with McTavish, Frobisher & Co. In an agreement dated September 26, 1789, Askin engaged to furnish the NWC annually for three successive years with six hundred bushels of hulled corn and twelve thousand pounds of flour. These goods were to be delivered to the NWC vessel at Detroit. In 1784, the NWC had finally been granted permission by Governor Haldimand to build its own ships for use on the Great Lakes. The vessel on which Askin was to ship the corn and flour was likely the sloop *Athabasca,* which had been built at Grand Portage in 1786. It was jointly owned by the part-ners of the NWC and a man named Daniel Sutherland. Sutherland and Askin gave a bond for £1,800, on the condition that if the said vessel was sent to any destination other than those specified on her pass, that sum would be forfeited.

≡:≡

IF THE NWC partners had little recreation when they were in the wilder-ness, they made up for it when they were in Montreal. The ultra-exclusive Beaver Club was founded in Montreal in 1785 by nineteen men who had all spent at least one winter working in the fur trade in the North West as young men. Later, membership was extended to fifty-five men with ten honorary members. The object of the meetings was "to bring together, at stated periods, during the winter season, a set of men highly respectable in Society, who had passed their best days in a savage country and had encountered the difficulties and dangers incident to a pursuit of the fur trade of Canada."[9] Over the life of the Beaver Club (1785–1827), it had approximately one hundred different members. Although membership was not reserved exclusively for Nor'Westers, HBC men were not allowed to become members until after 1821.

The founding members included Alexander Henry the Elder, the Frobisher brothers, and Peter Pond. The rules meant that McTavish, who had never wintered in the North West, was not actually eligible for membership, although he was finally invited to join in 1792. It seems reasonable to assume that the rules were broken for McTavish because of his prominence in the fur trade. However, some people claimed that he was only invited because he settled social accounts by fighting duels. According to one story, McTavish had fought a duel in Detroit in 1772 against a land speculator named William Constable. No details are known, but Constable was evidently in business with McTavish's friend William Edgar at one time, so McTavish and Constable quite likely knew each other. Another story claimed that a prominent Montreal physician named George Selby challenged McTavish to a duel because he had not been invited to one of McTavish's balls. McTavish, who was a crack shot, deliberately missed him. This latter story seems highly unlikely because Dr. Selby and McTavish were close friends. In fact, one of the terms of McTavish's will stated, "I give and bequeath to my friend Dr. George Selby the sum of two hundred pounds . . . as a mark of my esteem and regard." [10]

On admission to the Beaver Club, each member had a gold medal (referred to as a jewel) struck with his name, date of first winter in the North West, and the club motto, "Fortitude in Distress." The jewel was to be suspended from a blue ribbon and worn to all meetings. Failure to wear it meant a fine of one dollar. Most of the jewels had the same basic design: a beaver gnawing a tree and the words "Industry & Perseverance" on the obverse, and four men in a canoe and the club motto on the reverse.

Meetings were normally held fortnightly from December to April with occasional meetings held at other times. A club rule stated that "no member shall have a party at his house on club days, nor accept invitations; but if in town must attend, except prevented by indisposition." [11]

At each Beaver Club meeting, members passed around a calumet, or peace pipe, and offered toasts to the mother of all saints; the king; the fur trade in all its branches; voyageurs, wives, and children; and absent members. Dinner included such country foods as pemmican, roast beaver, sturgeon, and wild rice. Although the club had its own crested crystal

Simon McTavish owned this house at 27 St. Jean-Baptiste Street, Montreal. It was photographed in 1896. McCORD MUSEUM, MP-0000.228.1

and china with matching silverware, they never owned a clubhouse. They met at various hotels or public houses and occasionally in private homes. The bill for a Beaver Club dinner for thirty-two members and guests in September 1808 totalled £28.15. In addition to the food, the bill included more than sixty bottles of wine, twelve quarts of ale, an unspecified amount of hard liquor and negus (a kind of hot punch), cigars, pipes, tobacco, and payment for several broken wine glasses.[12]

The climax of a Beaver Club meeting was "The Grand Voyage." All present sat on the floor as though in a giant canoe and began to paddle, using swords, walking sticks, or even fire tongs as paddles. At the same time, they shouted out traditional voyageur songs.

The earliest existing minute books for the club are dated 1807. One of the items in the 1807 Beaver Club Minute Book listed names of five newly admitted members who received the same rights and privileges as the old members and were requested to provide themselves with gold medals accordingly. In order to be admitted to membership, a unanimous vote of the existing members was required. Rather surprisingly, immediately following their admittance, these new members said that they wished the name of the club be changed from the Beaver Club to the Voyageurs Club. When it was proposed to put the name change to a vote, "some altercation took place." One of the older members was so angry with that proposal that he "instantly retired from the club room" and apparently never attended another meeting. The vote was tied, with William McGillivray among those voting to keep the original name. As a result, they finally settled the issue by the toss of a dollar—heads for the original name, tails for the new name. The original name won.[13]

The membership list of the Beaver Club includes the names of almost all NWC partners who lived in Montreal. Invited guests included such well-known people as Sir John Franklin, Lord Selkirk, General Brock, and Washington Irving. William McGillivray, who was elected as a member in 1795, was an active and enthusiastic participant in Beaver Club festivities.

7 ROCKY NOR'WESTER RELATIONS, 1793—97

The Highlanders have fled New York for a Montreal canoe,
The Great Lakes, the black spruce, the Northwest Rendezvous
The voyageurs, the coureurs de bois, the Ojibwa and the Cree
They know how a man can fall . . . for the big lonely.

A gentleman, a partner, beaver pelts I trade,
Fort Kaministiquia will soon bear my name,
From a highland farm in the Scottish hills
To a prince on an inland sea.

— RODNEY BROWN, FROM "THE BIG LONELY"[1]

When William McGillivray returned to Montreal in 1793 on his way to a furlough in England and Scotland, both he and the city had greatly changed since his arrival there in the summer of 1784. The city had grown considerably. The NWC counting house was still at the intersection of St. Gabriel and Notre Dame Streets; however, McTavish, Frobisher & Co. had just completed a fine new stone warehouse on Vaudreuil Street, which they partially leased to John Jacob Astor. The date 1793 was chiselled over the door of the warehouse, which featured a steep peaked roof and was protected with iron shutters. The first Montreal post office had opened the previous year and offered twice-weekly mail service to the United States, which would have been welcomed by the NWC agents who had frequent business dealings in New York.

Many of McTavish's business friends and colleagues—including Alexander Henry, James McGill, Isaac Todd, and Joseph Frobisher—had either retired or were about to do so. Some were building fine mansions in the city or on Mont Royal. Joseph Frobisher was a particularly social man who kept a diary of all his dinner engagements up until weeks before his death in 1810. Frobisher and his wife entertained John Graves Simcoe, lieutenant-governor of Upper Canada, and Mrs. Simcoe on a number of occasions when they visited Montreal. Mrs. Simcoe found the view from Mont Royal "remarkably fine" and said that "the spires of the churches, covered with tin, give brilliancy to the scene and look like mosques." But when Frobisher took them for a drive toward Lachine one day, Mrs. Simcoe commented that she thought it was "merely to show how bad the road was."[2]

In 1783, the year McGillivray arrived in Canada, the NWC had employed about five hundred voyageurs, divided equally between les mangeurs de lard, who transported goods from Montreal to the Grand Portage, and les hommes du nord, who transported goods from Grand Portage to the interior posts of le pays d'en haut. By 1790, the Montreal to Grand Portage leg of the trip alone required 350 paddlers, and in 1802 the NWC employed approximately 1,500 French-Canadian servants.

Over his nine years in North America, William McGillivray had changed from an awkward youth to a confident young man in the prime of life. Before leaving on his furlough, he learned that he had been made a partner in McTavish, Frobisher & Co. and that he would take up his duties as an agent after his return in the summer of 1794. This was welcome news to the ambitious McGillivray, particularly since it meant that he would no longer have to spend his winters in the wilderness.

When he arrived in Montreal, McGillivray also learned that his forty-three-year-old uncle was shortly to be married to seventeen-year-old Marie Marguerite Chaboillez, daughter of McTavish's fur-trade colleague Charles Chaboillez. Although one source states that McTavish had a country wife at one time, there is no corroboration of this relationship. Even if he did have a country wife, it is unlikely that he had any surviving children with her. McTavish, who left bequests in his will to almost everyone even remotely related to him—and to many who were not—surely would have mentioned any such children in his will, even if he no longer had any connection with their mother.

One of the first things McGillivray did upon his arrival in Montreal was to buy new clothes for his uncle's wedding and the voyage to London. In later years, he had a reputation as a man who liked to wear expensive and fashionable clothes. At this time, however, it may have been simply that he had filled out from the slender youth he had been when he arrived from Scotland and no longer had any dress clothes that fit him.

Immediately after the wedding, McGillivray left on his furlough. He first travelled to Scotland and spent a month with his family. The countryside where he had grown up had changed little in the years he had been away, but his parents were the only members of his family who were still really familiar to him. Three married brothers and sisters lived nearby, and Duncan was already in North America. His remaining siblings —Simon, Betsy, Margery, and Mary—all of whom would later come to Canada, were still living at home. Next to seeing his family, another highlight of his visit to Scotland occurred in January when he was commanded to attend a reception at Inverness and was named an honorary burgess of the city.

After visiting his family, McGillivray went to London, where he visited his uncle Simon, who was spending his honeymoon there. He also called on Patrick Small, now a London merchant, and went shopping. An item in the account books of McTavish, Fraser & Co., dated March 24, 1794, is a bill for £30-8-7 (pounds, shillings, and pence) from Mr. McGillivray's tailor.

Though he may not have realized it at the time, the most significant event of McGillivray's furlough was a visit to the family of NWC apprentice John McDonald of Garth. While delivering John's messages, McGillivray became acquainted with his sister Magdalen. McGillivray returned to North America in the spring of 1794 to take up his duties as an agent but returned to London that fall to spend his second consecutive winter there. It seems likely that Magdalen McDonald was the reason for a second trip to Britain so soon after his furlough.

AS A NEWLY minted agent, William McGillivray was learning more about the broader workings of the NWC than he had experienced as a clerk or even after he became a wintering partner. It is difficult in today's world of virtually instantaneous communications and rapid air travel to realize how slowly transnational businesses like the NWC operated in the 1790s. The following chart compiled by Alexander Mackenzie shows this clearly:

October 1796	Order for trade goods sent to London from Montreal
March 1797	Goods shipped from London
June 1797	Goods arrive in Montreal
Winter 1797–98	Goods packed for shipment by canoe to northwest
May 1798	Goods sent from Montreal to northwest
Summer 1798	Goods arrive at Grand Portage and sent to posts
Winter 1798–99	Goods are traded for furs
Spring 1799	Furs shipped to Grand Portage
September 1799	Furs arrive Montreal
Fall 1799	Furs shipped to London
Spring 1800	Furs sold
Summer 1800	Furs paid for

Mackenzie concluded his chart by observing that the slow return on investment in the fur trade "makes this a very heavy business." [3]

Traditionally, the furs were sold in London at public auction, but in the 1790s McTavish, Fraser & Co. (the London firm) began attempting to connect directly with possible buyers. McTavish consigned a shipment of furs to a German buyer named Schneider. These furs did not reach their destination, as the ship carrying them ran aground on the coast of the Netherlands. The furs were salvaged and sold in London, with Schneider allowed his pickings of the cargo. Fraser wrote to McTavish in May 1792, "Consulted our landlord about the German furriers. He seems to think he can get the business managed for me; if so I shall like it better than to apply to Schneider or any of the traders as it might excite jealousies and apprehensions." [4]

It seems likely that Fraser was successful in making contact directly with German furriers because the connection with Schneider came to

Fur trader and explorer Sir Alexander Mackenzie was an important early partner in the NWC. LIBRARY AND ARCHIVES CANADA ACCESSION NO. 1990-553, E010957264

a hostile end less than six months later. James Hallowell, accountant and partner in McTavish, Frobisher & Co. (the Montreal firm), wrote to McTavish in January 1793 that "Robertson [apparently an agent] is not the kind of man Schneider would have chosen for his agent, but on the other hand the rage . . . of Schneider may have urged him to act in a manner we think inconsistent with his own interests."[5] The details of what happened to enrage Schneider are unknown.

The stranded cargo ship was not the only problem during this period. In May 1794, the partners in Montreal wrote collectively to McTavish in response to a letter he had sent to them, with a duplicate copy to Fraser. In the letter, the partners reminded McTavish and Fraser of the sacrifices they had made and then promised that they would "cheerfully" make other sacrifices "for the promotion of our common interests and the preservation of our common credit."[6] They did not, however, honour the request for funds that was the reason for McTavish's letter in the first place.

McTavish made an emotional response to this letter on August 7, 1794:

From what I have written to Mr. Frobisher in reply to his letter . . . you may judge of my mortification and disappointment this morning on receiving a copy of your letter of the 31st of May wherein you explicitly confirmed the termination he appeared to have adopted under your individual signatures. Really sirs, I am quite confounded at such inconsiderate conduct on your part and was not everything at stake, I should not be sorry to see you suffer for your obstinacy. How you could think the bills McGillivray had drawn . . . should render it unnecessary for you to send home what was so particularly recommended to you after the fullest explanation of the necessity of so doing . . . and I can only say it is very hard after so many years of anxious and unwearied application . . . that you will not give me credit now for knowing what our situation on this side of the water requires better than you can do at such a distance . . . I shall go out in the spring and take a part in the future deliberation on the management of the business in Canada.[7]

James Hallowell responded with an equally emotional letter on November 17, 1794:

You say you "must consider the letter of 31st of May as mine, altho' it appears <u>sanctioned</u> by the signatures of the other partners" . . . I am shocked at the meaning conveyed in that expression . . . Every letter I have written . . . has been communicated to Mr. Frobisher & Mr. Gregory & by them approved . . . Your letter is particularly severe & has most sensibly affected me. I have lived in the habit of sacrificing my opinions and my feelings to yours, for which, however, I must confess, I expected some credit with you. You, I am afraid, have placed this deference to a wrong account—to a meanness of spirit on my part and to the want of having an opinion of my own, when the true principles which governed my conduct were a sense of obligation to, & personal regard for you—and more than all, a strong persuasion that that regard was reciprocal.

. . . In the spring I hope we shall see you, which will relieve me in a situation where, subordinate to everyone, you seem to hold me accountable for all.

Sincerely yours, James Hallowell [8]

It is not clear why Hallowell and McTavish were both so unhappy with their business relationship at this time and why the partners refused to send money that McTavish felt was crucial to the business. It is possible that they felt that McTavish was spending too much time enjoying himself with his young wife instead of tending to business in Montreal, and some of them did not approve of William's promotion. By this time, many Nor'Westers considered that McTavish had become the arrogant "Marquis" or "Premier" who favoured relatives to the detriment of other NWC employees and partners. McTavish had planned to make his home in England after his marriage and manage the fur-trade business from London; however, he changed his mind because his wife was homesick for Montreal and possibly also because of his partners' disapproval.

McTavish and the other senior partners were not the only ones having trouble. The 1794 rendezvous at Grand Portage, McGillivray's first meeting as an apprentice agent, was a baptism of fire. He must have been aware that his promotion had been met with envy or bitterness by some of his fellow winterers, who thought that he had been promoted due to family connections ahead of more deserving traders. As Duncan McGillivray wrote to their uncle, "One great cause for discontent among some of the winterers is my brother's present situation in Montreal . . . I am exceedingly glad it exempts him from the troubles and dangers of the N.W." [9]

The 1794 rendezvous was also made difficult for McGillivray because of McTavish's long absence in London. Angus Shaw, who would later become McGillivray's brother-in-law, wrote to McTavish about this issue. He began by saying how pleased he was with William's promotion. Though his friends "will feel the loss of his abilities greatly, yet I have every reason to suppose that loss will be partly if not wholly supplied by his activity and steadiness at this place where such a character has been so much wanted since you abandoned us." Another visit here from "you would in my opinion be of great service to the concern in general" because the winterers required closer leadership. [10]

Among the dissatisfied Nor'Westers in 1794 was a depressed Alexander Mackenzie. He wrote to his cousin Roderick from Fort Chipewyan in January of that year:

> *I wish we could contrive matters so that we could both go to the Portage . . . I am fully bent upon going down, for I think it unpardonable for anybody to remain in this country who can leave it. What a pretty situation I am in this winter, starving and alone . . . even my own servant is equal to the performance of my winter occupation, and the profits, I am afraid, will be so small . . . that it will not be worth any man's while to remain in it.*[11]

Today, the following words painted on a rock near the Pacific coast are considered to be of huge significance in Canadian history: "Alexander Mackenzie from Canada by land, July 22, 1793." However, this was not the case in the 1790s. Neither Mackenzie's route to the Pacific nor the one he followed to the Arctic Ocean was of immediate practical use to the NWC. On his way to Montreal in the fall of 1794, Mackenzie shared his ideas for reorganizing the fur trade with Lieutenant-Governor Simcoe of Upper Canada. He proposed that the NWC, the HBC, and the East India Company should participate in a co-operative venture into the Pacific trade before the Americans became any more powerful in that field.

Upon his arrival in Montreal, Mackenzie discussed his ideas with Joseph Frobisher and acted as a spokesman for the younger NWC partners. He told Frobisher that the younger partners were very dissatisfied both with the size of their shares as set out in the NWC agreement of 1792 and with the quality of the trade goods they received. Mackenzie suggested that an extra share be allowed for each of seven young partners who already had one share each. As well, two shares should be allowed for an eighth man who was not currently a partner.

Frobisher reported in detail to McTavish on his interview with Mackenzie and told McTavish that he agreed with Mackenzie's proposal regarding the extra shares because this would relieve the company of paying salaries for these men. The result was the Agreement of 1795. As in the 1792 agreement, the company was divided into forty-six shares. The major difference between the two agreements was that the number of shares held by McTavish, Frobisher & Co., which was twenty in 1792, was reduced to fourteen in 1795. The other notable change was that four shares in the 1795 agreement were not issued to anyone and would only be disposed of if necessary.[12]

Simon McTavish had mixed feelings about Mackenzie's ideas. It was in his self-interest to keep Montreal dominant in the fur trade, but there would also be economic benefits in having a Pacific port and access to Hudson Bay. McTavish had earlier unsuccessfully appealed to British prime minister William Pitt for the repeal of the HBC charter, but when Pitt pointed out that such a change would require an Act of Parliament, an expensive and time-consuming exercise, McTavish had given up the idea.

In the mid-1790s, the NWC was also vitally concerned about boundary issues. The Treaty of Paris, which ended the American Revolution, was signed in 1783; however, the boundary line between British North America and the United States was not finalized until Jay's Treaty was signed in 1794. Despite their strong interest in the issue, the Nor'Westers were not consulted during the Jay's Treaty negotiations. According to the terms of the treaty, Britain agreed to give up its military posts in the United States by June 1796. In return, Article III of the treaty stipulated that Aboriginals were allowed to freely cross the Canada–US border; therefore, Montreal traders could still obtain furs from Aboriginals in the upper Mississippi Valley, although the United States could levy customs duties on British goods entering the country. As the treaty put it, Canadians and Americans were to have equal rights to "navigate all the lakes, rivers and waters . . . and freely to carry on trade and commerce with each other."[13] No duties were to be charged on goods carried over the Grand Portage; however, American customs officials ruled that only large kegs of rum could be carried across the technically duty-free portage. Because large kegs could not be carried in the smaller northern canoes used beyond Grand Portage, use of the portage became almost impossible. Thus it became imperative to find an alternative portage on the British side of the border.

McGillivray had previously met David Thompson, the Welsh-born HBC trader and explorer, and formed a good opinion of him. Thompson, who was frustrated with the HBC's lack of support for his explorations, sought employment with the NWC when his contract with the HBC was up for renewal in 1797. He was just the man McGillivray was looking for.

Even though the boundary between the United States and British North America had been set along the forty-ninth parallel, no one seemed to know exactly where that was. McGillivray hired Thompson to determine the location of the new boundary line and find out on which side of the border certain NWC posts were located.

The NWC signed a five-year agreement in 1796 with Jean-Baptiste Cadotte Jr. to carry on trade in the Fond du Lac area, and a second agreement was made with Cadotte in 1803. Cadotte's father, Jean-Baptiste Sr., had been a Canadian fur trader in the Sault Ste. Marie area on what became the American side of the border. The agreements with Cadotte Jr., who was born in American territory and lived there for much of his life, were made in an effort to evade some of the new regulations restricting Canadian trade over the forty-ninth parallel. This proved so successful that trade with American posts actually increased for a time.

—≣:≣—

IN DECEMBER OF 1797, Colonel George Landmann of the Corps of Royal Engineers arrived in Montreal and became acquainted with many Nor'Westers, including McGillivray and Alexander Mackenzie. Mackenzie was acting as assistant to McGillivray at this time, and the two men shared a house. Landmann found Montrealers very hospitable. "I had not been 24 hours at Montreal before I was invited to dine . . . every day . . . during a week or ten days," he wrote.[14] Landmann described in detail one notable party held a few days after Christmas to which he was invited by Mackenzie and McGillivray. Although Landmann does not say so, it seems likely that this was a regular gathering of the Beaver Club. The party of about twenty men dined at 4 PM. After dining and taking perhaps a bottle of wine each, the married men retired, leaving about a dozen men who then began to celebrate in true Highland style. As Landmann wrote, "By four o'clock in the morning, the whole of us had arrived at such a degree of perfection that we could all give the war-whoop as well as Mackenzie and McGillivray, we could all sing admirably, we could all drink like fishes, and we all thought we could dance on the table without disturbing a single [piece of the glassware] . . . by which it was profusely covered." They soon discovered that "was a complete delusion." They broke all the glassware on the table, and the heads and hands of the party suffered "many severe contusions, cuts, and scratches." Landmann afterward learned that 120 bottles of wine had been consumed, but he thought "a great deal had been spilt."[15]

In late April, Landmann received orders to go to St. Joseph Island in Lake Huron, a vital gateway to Lake Superior, which the British had fortified in 1796. St. Joseph's Island was to replace Michilimackinac as an NWC post, since the latter was now on the American side of the border. McGillivray, who was travelling to the summer rendezvous, offered Landmann passage in his canoe. They travelled by calèche from Montreal to Lachine on May 12, the earliest possible day to avoid ice. The nine-mile trip took three hours because the road was scattered with large stones and puddles of water that concealed many deep holes. At Lachine, they found lunch ready in a house belonging to the NWC. The guests included several army officers and some Nor'Westers who were not going with the brigade. Everyone but Landmann was Highland born. The lunch was followed by drinking, speeches, reminiscences, and farewells "with the deoch an dorus"[16] over and over again. By six or seven o'clock, Landmann, like many others, had fallen from his chair. He crawled into an unused fireplace to avoid being trampled. Eventually, Mackenzie and McGillivray were the only two men still sitting. Mackenzie proposed they drink to the memory of the fallen and give a war whoop over them. In attempting to push the bottle to McGillivray at the opposite end of the table, Mackenzie slid off his chair. At the same time, McGillivray reached for the bottle and slid helplessly to the floor.

While this celebration was going on, the NWC clerks sent the canoes and baggage to the end of the island and made arrangements for the others to follow by land, which they did not do until about 9 PM. They travelled most of the night in strong wind and drizzling rain, frequently being dumped out into ditches or pools of water. The revellers finally arrived at the end of the island about 6 AM—all looking and feeling much the worse for wear. Landmann described his head as strongly resembling "a mop which had been first dipped into water and then into a dust-hole."[17]

They were given only a brief time to recover before the voyageurs were ordered to embark and they continued on their journey—McGillivray to the 1798 summer rendezvous and Landmann to St. Joseph Island.

8 VIOLENCE AND THE NEW NORTH WEST COMPANY, 1798–1806

As faithful friends do depart,
A wasted bond, which has been spun,
Weakened, battered and undone,
And always vengeance in the way

. . .

Wishing things could mend and heal,
But anger is all they wish to feel,
Scared to admit that they may long
To one day fix the things gone wrong.

FROM "BROKEN FRIENDSHIP" (ANONYMOUS)

Between the mid-1790s and 1804, there was increasing violence in the Northwest fur trade. The Nor'Westers didn't approve of any competition, either from the HBC or from independent companies. Traders who dared to oppose the NWC were hampered by vindictive actions. Nor'Westers felled huge trees to block competitors' access to streams and portages and destroyed their trade goods and equipment. They convinced Native people by threats or bribes not to trade for food with NWC competitors. Most Nor'Westers appeared to believe that all was fair in love and trade war.

Two of the companies opposing the NWC on the Saskatchewan were Forsyth, Richardson & Co. of Detroit, and Parker, Gerrard & Ogilvy of Montreal. The competition between the two was ruinous. As a result, the New Northwest Company was officially formed in October 1798 when these two companies and several smaller firms joined together. The New Northwest Company was commonly known as the XY Company because of the way they marked their bales of fur. It was also sometimes referred to as the Little Company and its men as "potties," because that had been the nickname used for Forsyth, Richardson & Co. and its employees. "Potties" may be an English rendering of *petits* or come from the expression la petite potée, a collection of things or people of small value.[1] Duncan McGillivray was particularly aggressive in opposing competitors. In the summer of 1802, Paul Harvieux, an employee of two Michilimackinac traders, arrived in the Grand Portage area with a canoe-load of trade goods and an American trading licence in accordance with Jay's Treaty. Harvieux set up several tents for trading. Almost immediately Duncan demanded that Harvieux move his tents. Before Harvieux had a chance to take any action, however, Duncan drew a hunting knife and slashed one of the tents. Several other Nor'Westers then rushed in to knock down the tents, and one threatened to break Harvieux's neck. At the same time, a servant tore to bits a tent that Harvieux just had sold to an NWC engagé and burned it. Duncan then ordered the engagés not to have any dealings with Harvieux.

Although Harvieux continued to trade as best he could, he maintained that his trade was considerably reduced by the threats. As a result, his employers sued Duncan McGillivray. The Court of King's Bench in Montreal found McGillivray guilty on April 5, 1804, and sentenced him to pay five hundred pounds in damages to the plaintiffs, plus court costs.

In another incident, Duncan unsuccessfully attempted to kidnap three former NWC employees now working for the XY Company. A young clerk with the XY Company wrote that NWC men were also suspected of boring gimlet holes in thirty kegs of high wine while the XY men were having a regale. (High wine was very strong West Indian rum that was diluted with water before sale or distribution by fur traders.) According to the clerk, the Nor'Westers called such actions "witty tricks."[2]

By the early 1800s, the rivalry between the old and new North West Companies had become so intense and violent that the situation was near civil war on the Saskatchewan, and the fur trade was being seriously harmed. The violence was fuelled by a large increase in the consumption of liquor. In 1800, the NWC ordered 10,098 gallons of liquor; in 1803, this amount increased to 16,299 gallons, and the traders in opposition ordered 5,000 gallons.[3]

As a result, the British government ("in compliance with a petition from Canada") passed an act known as the Canada Jurisdiction Act on August 11, 1803. It provided that offences committed in the Indian Territories should be tried in the same manner and be liable to the same punishments as offences that occurred in Canada. It empowered the Governor of Lower Canada to name Justices of the Peace for Indian Territories. These justices had authority to bring men to Canada from the North West to be tried in Lower Canadian courts. Those selected to enforce the law were hardly unbiased, however. The first group of justices named were all fur traders, including William and Duncan McGillivray, Roderick McKenzie, and Alexander Mackenzie.[4]

Alexander Mackenzie had continued to be dissatisfied with his treatment by the NWC and became leader of a group of younger wintering partners. At the 1799 rendezvous, and with his contract up for renewal, Mackenzie announced that he was leaving the NWC. A heated discussion ensued between the wintering partners and the Montreal agents. The partners declared that Mackenzie alone had their confidence and urged him not to resign; but McTavish sat in silence, refusing to add his voice to those urging Mackenzie to stay. At that, Mackenzie stalked out of the meeting. He later confessed that he had been so angry that he forgot "that which we seldom lose sight of," his self-interest.[5] He retired from the NWC in November and soon afterward joined the XY Co.

William McGillivray wrote to wintering partner Æneas Cameron in September 1799 about Mackenzie's actions:

> He has realized a handsome sum of money and quits a very troublesome business—but at the present juncture we could wish he still retained his situation as we cannot be too strong. This has obliged us to take my brother Duncan from the NWest. He has resigned his share and will go up to assist me yearly at the Grand Portage to manage the business.[6]

McGillivray wrote a second letter to Cameron regarding Mackenzie in May 1800:

I sincerely hope when he has conversed with men of more experience and cooler heads than his own, he will find it equally desirable to terminate the matter amicably . . . Hard indeed it would be on us all, on me particularly, *if after our long intimacy, we could only look on each other as enemies in future.*[7]

Duncan McGillivray judged Mackenzie much more harshly than did William. He wrote to Cameron that some "very unwarrantable measures" were adopted in an attempt to retain Mackenzie. Duncan was also very critical of Angus Shaw for using Mackenzie as a tool to excite indignation against the NWC, even though Shaw hated Mackenzie. According to Duncan, Shaw's motive was disappointment "in ill-founded pretensions of becoming a partner" in the NWC himself.[8] Shaw was engaged to William and Duncan's sister Margery and married her in 1802. Although the McGillivray brothers did not have a very high opinion of Shaw's business ability, he did become a partner in 1806.

Because so many Nor'Westers were related to each other or shared close friendships, the split that resulted in the formation of the New North West Company was much closer to a family breakup than a business one. Roderick McKenzie found it especially difficult when he was asked to fill the NWC vacancy created by Alexander Mackenzie's resignation. "I accepted, though with great reluctance," he wrote.[9] Because Roderick and Alexander had enjoyed such a close relationship both personally and professionally, Roderick realized that Alexander expected him to leave the NWC as well. Alexander was both disappointed and displeased when Roderick did not do so. The two men did not resume their regular correspondence until five years later, after the union of the NWC and the New NWC in 1804. Even then, however, they were not on the same intimate footing as before. Instead of addressing his cousin as "Roderick" or "Rory," Alexander now began letters to him with "Dear Sir."[10]

Alexander Henry the Elder wrote his observations about the formation of the XY Company to John Askin in January 1799, noting that the split had raised wages considerably and that young men wanted to sign contracts for only a year instead of three or four. "The old NWC is all in the hands of McTavish. Frobisher and McKenzie are out. The latter went off in a pet. The cause, as far as I can learn, was who should be the first—McTavish or McK—and as there could not be two Caesars in Rome, one must remove."[11] McTavish was so bitter against the Nor'Westers who supported Mackenzie that he refused to resume personal correspondence with them. On April 20, 1800, McTavish wrote a joint letter to the wintering partners at Grand Portage:

> *I have been in the yearly habit of addressing several of [you] . . .*
> *individually . . . and thereby cultivate a friendship that I thought to*
> *be reciprocal . . . From the occurrences that passed at the Portage*
> *last summer, I am sorry to find that I must for the future abridge*
> *my correspondence in that quarter . . . You cannot be surprised*
> *that after so many years of the most zealous attachment and . . .*
> *successful exertion in promoting the interests of the . . . NWC,*
> *I feel hurt at the distrust and want of confidence that appeared*
> *throughout all your deliberations last season, and particularly*
> *at the attempt which was made to dictate to my house in the*
> *appointment of its agents at the portage, which interference on*
> *your part is not warranted by our contract with you.*[12]

It seems fair to say that Mackenzie and McTavish shared the blame for the break between them. Historian Elaine Allan Mitchell wrote of Mackenzie, "His youth, pride, and comparative inexperience in business led him to place himself in an untenable position which McTavish soon turned to his own advantage." On the other hand, had McTavish "recognized the young man's achievements as they deserved and shown an interest in his ideas, even if he could not subscribe to them, perhaps the misunderstanding need never have arisen."[13]

During this tumultuous period, the NWC was also feuding with the HBC. The following correspondence between HBC factor William Tomison and McGillivray gives some indication of the level of animosity that existed between the two companies. When Tomison protested an action of the Nor'Westers by which he believed the HBC lost ninety beaver, McGillivray replied sharply. He wrote in June 1792 that Tomison was calling "a man of character" a robber "although he has done nothing but what is conformable to the customs of the country from time immemorial, and what I am certain many of your Honourable Company servants have done." He went on to say that the Nor'Westers lost almost two thousand beaver to the HBC in a similar situation several years earlier.[14]

Tomison also wrote from Edmonton House to Duncan McGillivray in 1798 that he had been informed by several Bungee Indians that McGillivray had seized furs with which the Bungee had planned to pay their credits to the HBC. Tomison charged that during the current season the Nor'Westers had intercepted not less than five hundred beaver that rightfully were property of the HBC. He concluded his letter by saying that he was sending three men to collect the HBC property. "If refused I shall be induced to report you to the Honourable HBC as gentlemen of the first rank." Tomison was known as a very stern, humourless, and hot-tempered man, and it's possible this comment was intended sarcastically. There is no indication that any further action was taken on this charge.[15]

In another disagreement, the HBC wrote "requiring a boat to be returned" which they charged had been " forcibly detained" by Alexander Henry the Younger from one of their men the previous September, and enquiring whether such conduct was or was not contrary to McGillivray's directions. McGillivray replied that, so far as he could determine from the testimony of those present, the two men had willingly exchanged a boat and a canoe. Thus Henry had every right to keep the boat. He then defended himself: "With regard to myself (or I presume you mean the NWC) authorizing violent and illegal acts in the people they employ— Our conduct . . . clearly proves the contrary." He continued the letter by saying that he hoped to meet someone from the HBC with whom he could discuss the tract of country fitted out from Moose Fort by both the NWC and the HBC. "An arrangement in my opinion could be made which would be beneficial to both parties by withdrawing many posts at present occupied where the natives are the only gainers."[16]

Simon McTavish and his nephew Duncan made several unsuccessful attempts to persuade the HBC to allow the NWC to bring in goods via Hudson Bay. In an attempt to have the matter settled in court, McTavish had Duncan send a letter to the HBC "begging them to sue him for what he is going to do."[17] Then, in the spring of 1803, McTavish sent the 150-ton vessel *Beaver* to trade on Hudson Bay. That same year, he also rented southern Labrador for one thousand pounds a year in response to the HBC's attempts to bar other traders from Labrador. He hired Captain John Richards, formerly employed by the HBC, and sent him and an NWC partner on the ship *Eddystone* to establish a trading post at Charlton Island on James Bay. They claimed the island for the NWC, even though it was in HBC territory. They built one fort on the island and two other forts at the mouths of the Moose and Eastmain Rivers but had little financial success and soon abandoned these posts. The HBC presented their case against the NWC to legal officials, who gave the opinion that the HBC title was valid and that the NWC had trespassed; however, because it was not a criminal action, there was no recourse to English courts. This was certainly a disappointment to the NWC.

Meanwhile, the NWC continued its attempts to stymie competitors whenever possible. When assignments were given out to the wintering partners at the 1806 rendezvous, partner Alexander McKay was told "to watch Delorme,"[18] a trader attempting to compete with the NWC by way of Grand Portage. In order to carry out his task, McKay was assigned a clerk, two guides, and two canoes. McKay and his engagés forced Delorme to abandon his trade efforts by cutting down trees to block his portage route.

In around 1804, after NWC trader François Malhiot gave a chief named Moose's Nose a set of chief's clothing, he harangued Moose's Nose on the importance of trading only with the NWC:

> *I would like very much to forget what you did last year and believe that it was not your fault that we did not receive all your furs. But do not do the same in the future. The suit I give you today should show you the road you must follow. I rely on all your promises. Do not deceive me . . . I not only want your furs, but also your wheat [wild rice] . . . My orders from our father [William McGillivray] were . . . I was not to give you anything this fall and wait until I knew you. But after what you have just told me . . . I feel obliged to do what I have just done. Take courage then and think of your fort [the NWC fort].*[19]

In 1804, Nor'Wester Duncan Cameron visited the HBC's Fort Osnaburgh in Northern Ontario, about twenty kilometres south of the modern community Pickle Lake, and wrote a fascinating account of the relationship between the NWC and the HBC during the early years of the nineteenth century. Goodwin, the man in charge of Osnaburgh, invited the Nor'Westers to spend the night because of a violent storm with heavy showers. Two Native trappers arrived soon after. Cameron was anxious to talk to them, "but it was very difficult, as they were strictly watched by the interpreter." Obviously Goodwin did not want the Nor'Westers talking privately to these men. Finally, Cameron managed to speak to one man long enough to invite them both to come to his tent the next day because he wished to make them a present. Cameron was defensive about issuing this invitation:

People unacquainted with the nature of the Indian trade will reckon my behaviour very rude and say that I made very ungrateful returns for the polite hospitality I received. I admit that I am not entirely reconciled to the propriety of the conduct, although it is a very common custom in this country, which nothing but the nature of the trade can excuse.[20]

According to Cameron, the next morning the two trappers were lying "dead drunk, after having been troublesome and insolent to the English the whole night. These people [the English] have the patience of Job and are real slaves to the Indians who come to their forts. We [Nor'Westers] keep them at greater distance, which makes them more respectful to us than to the English."[21] Cameron's view in this matter is the complete opposite of the commonly held view that the Nor'Westers treated Native peoples with more equity than did the HBC traders.[22]

To Cameron's surprise, the two trappers did finally arrive at his camp, and he gave each man a glass of shrub. The men said that "the English were too pitiful to have such a chief's liquor as that." While that comment would merely be part of negotiating tactics, Cameron went on to say that the English treated the Native people "much better than we could afford to do, but they had not the art of convincing the Indians of that."[23] This statement is also contrary to the accepted view.

Cameron told the trappers that if they brought their furs to him rather than to the English, "I would make them a present of their old debts [from the previous winter]. Nothing was lost by the promise, as I was quite sure that we would never see a skin's worth of these old credits." Then he gifted them with a two-gallon keg of high wine and three fathoms of tobacco and told them to pass this message on to the rest of their family and friends.[24]

Cameron later met a group of Natives, including a man known as "Cotton Shirt" who asked that he leave a trader in their area. Cotton Shirt said that this was the only area where a few beaver remained, and there were plenty of whitefish to sustain them over the winter. "It is a general complaint in the whole department that beaver is getting very scarce," Cameron noted. He also said that Cotton Shirt was "very faithful to me these several years past . . . [and] is, without exception, the best hunter in the whole department." If a man is a good hunter and has "the usual large stock of impudence . . . with a little cunning, you must make a chief of him to secure his hunt; otherwise your opponents will debauch him from you, and you are sure to lose him."[25]

Cameron concluded that competition among the various trading groups was harmful to the traders. "The consequence will be that the Indians will get all they want for half the value and laugh at them all . . . If no arrangements take place soon to prevent this squandering and put the trade on a better footing, it will require but a very short time to sink more money than has been gained in the country for several years back."[26]

—⯈:⯇—

IT IS NOT clear how many people normally lived at Grand Portage over the winter, since most of those associated with the NWC were only there during the summer. One trader noted that in July 1793 there were nearly one thousand NWC men at the post, resulting in a food shortage when the NWC ship *Otter* was late in arriving with expected supplies. Alexander Mackenzie believed that nothing but potatoes could be grown in the area because it was too cool and damp; however, there was an abundance of hay for feeding the cattle that were kept at the post for both meat and milk. Usually, one year's supply of food was kept on hand over the winter.

McGillivray was at Grand Portage frequently in summer during his first years as an agent. On June 9, 1795, on his way from Montreal to Grand Portage, he wrote McTavish that he had met *Otter* at Sault Ste. Marie on June 1. The crew of *Otter*, which had left Grand Portage on May 6, reported that the people at the post were all well and that one trader had already sent eleven thousand pièces across the portage. In 1798, McGillivray worked out the amount of provisions needed for all the posts for one year. He calculated that for Grand Portage alone, 1,080 bushels of corn were required for summer, plus 300 more for winter. This was out of a total of 4,000 bushels needed beyond Grand Portage. As well, Grand Portage required 260 bags of flour for summer and 50 for winter.

Because Jay's Treaty left Grand Portage on the American side of the border, its days as an NWC post were numbered. Roderick McKenzie was returning from Grand Portage to Lac la Pluie in the spring of 1798 when he met a Native family from whom he learned of the existence of another route parallel to the Grand Portage route. It began at the site of the old French post at the mouth of the Kaministiquia River. The land was very low and poorly drained, but otherwise it had four important factors in its favour: It was a direct link to the northwest via Lac la Pluie; it had an excellent harbour on Lake Superior; it was navigable for large canoes; and, above all, it was on British soil. McKenzie immediately wrote to McTavish about his discovery.

McTavish was delighted with McKenzie's letter, finding "much satis-faction and information" in it. "Your observations of the proposed road . . . convince me, beyond a doubt, that it would be more advantageous and easy for us than the Grand Portage, and . . . I think no time should be lost in moving our place of rendezvous."[27]

Despite McTavish's enthusiastic reaction, no one was really happy about moving the NWC headquarters. The NWC soon entered into an agreement with the local Ojibwa and Cree people (the Anishinabe), who gave the NWC a strip of land five miles wide on either side of the Kaministiquia River, stretching for twelve miles from Lake Superior. In exchange, the Anishinabe received three pounds in provincial cur-rency and "divers other good causes and valuable considerations."[28] The agreement was signed by ten Anishinabe "chiefs and old men" and Nor'Westers including Simon McTavish, Joseph Frobisher, William McGillivray, and Alexander Mackenzie. To make the agreement offi-cial, the Anishinabe gave the Nor'Westers a wampum belt and both groups signed a parchment document. Ten years later, the government told the NWC that the agreement had no legality because the law forbade the sale of Indian lands to anyone but the Crown. Despite this, it does not appear that the government took any action to return the land to the Anishinabe.

The voyageurs' contracts obliged them to perform six days of mandatory labour per year in addition to their regular duties. This allowed McTavish to order the voyageurs to drain the land where the new fort was to be built. This free labour reduced the cost of the new fort to about ten thousand pounds sterling. No plans for the fort have been located, but it is known that McGillivray directed the construction.

The final meeting at Grand Portage took place in 1802. The 1802 rendezvous was also the last time Simon McTavish visited the Great Lakes. A record number of partners—five Montreal agents and twenty-three winterers—were in attendance. The meeting was a sombre one because the NWC had lost Grand Portage and was unlikely to be recompensed by the Americans for its loss.

Montreal clerks trained in accounting attended the NWC's annual rendezvous to analyze the accounts brought in by the wintering partners. According to the 1802 agreement, the Montreal agents also brought a complete set of books to the rendezvous for the wintering partners to examine. Each partner had his portion of the year's outfit charged against his account and his returns credited to it. NWC bookkeeping was made very complex because of the slow pace of conducting transatlantic business and the confusing number of currencies used. Payments for an outfit's returns could take four years or more to be credited to a partner, as shown in Alexander Mackenzie's chart in Chapter 7.

Alexander Henry the Younger's accounts for the 1802 Lower Red River Outfit show the different currencies used in conducting NWC business. Costs incurred in Canada were given in Halifax currency, which was tied to sterling but had a lower value. The cost of goods from England and the sale of furs in England were shown in sterling. Transactions with the French in Lower Canada were in livres. Finally, North West or Grand Portage livres were used for the men's wages and expenses in the interior.

During construction of the new post, McGillivray was also involved with making transportation improvements. The major improvement took place at Sault Ste. Marie in 1797, when operations were transferred across the St. Mary's River from the American side to British territory. At that time, the NWC hired men to dig a canal 2,580 feet long and had the first lock on the Great Lakes constructed. The lock was thirty-eight feet long, designed to raise or lower one large canoe by nine feet.

Like McTavish in his younger years, McGillivray enjoyed visiting New York and made fairly frequent business trips there. In January 1799, he and Isaac Todd went to New York in connection with business dealings between the NWC and John Jacob Astor. Astor entertained the two men lavishly and took them to the theatre to see a hit Ben Jonson comedy.

While in New York, McGillivray and Todd rented a building in which to open a New York branch office for the NWC. McGillivray had realized in recent years that McTavish often seemed tired and increasingly quick-tempered, thus he felt it necessary to deal more deferentially with him than he had done previously. As a result, he wrote a detailed description of the building to McTavish—something he would not have considered doing a few years earlier. When McGillivray had first heard winterers refer to McTavish as "the Marquis," he had considered it as a term of respect. He soon realized, however, that it was quite the opposite.

=≡:≡=

ALONG WITH HIS considerable responsibilities to the NWC during this period, in 1800, William McGillivray took on a new role in his private life. Although no record of their meeting exists, McGillivray and Magdalen McDonald almost certainly met during his trip to London in the winter of 1793–94 when he delivered letters from her brother John McDonald of Garth to his family. As far as is known, there are no existing letters written by either William or Magdalen to each other, and no records of comments McGillivray made about her. But we do get a glimpse of Magdalen courtesy of Alexander Mackenzie. Despite the fact that he had already resigned from the NWC, Mackenzie was a guest at the McGillivray–McDonald wedding and sent a description of the bride to his cousin Roderick:

> *I must say something to you of Miss McDonald. She is an agreeable, lively brunette, of a most expressive countenance, middle stature, possessed in a superior degree of that pleasing familiarity which very soon would induce a stranger to think he had acquired a preference in her esteem, particularly if he is inclined to be vain*

himself. This talent in her appears natural, therefore you cannot state her a coquette . . . She is a very charming woman.[29]

Two days before the wedding, McGillivray formally settled six thousand pounds on his wife-to-be in a ceremony held at the London home of her brother Angus. On December 22, 1800, they were married in the tiny Anglican church of St. Mary le Bone. After the wedding, the couple honeymooned in Scotland, where they visited McGillivray's childhood home and his family members still living in the area. They also visited Edinburgh, where Magdalen had lived with her aunt as a child.

On March 4, 1801, McGillivray received a grant of arms at the Court of the Lord Lyon King of Arms in Princes Street in Edinburgh. His arms did not bear the ancient motto of the Clans McGillivray and Chattan, "Touch not the cat bot a glove." Instead he used the motto "Be mindful" from the Clan Campbell of Cawdor. McGillivray admired the current Lord of Cawdor, who had recently distinguished himself in battle with the French, and his wife was related to the Campbells. With this grant of arms, like his uncle, Simon McTavish, William had truly become part of the new North American aristocracy.

9 DEATHS AND OTHER CHANGES, 1804−11

For we are the same things our fathers have been,
We see the same sights that our fathers have seen,
We drink the same stream, and we feel the same sun
And we run the same course that our fathers have run.

The thoughts we are thinking our fathers would think,
From the death we are shrinking from they too would shrink,
To the life we are clinging to, they too would cling.

⟹ WILLIAM KNOX, FROM "MORTALITY" ⟸

William McGillivray was at the 1804 annual rendezvous when a guide arrived by light canoe with a letter informing him that Simon McTavish had died on July 6 while supervising construction of his mansion on Mont Royal. McGillivray left immediately for Montreal to take care of both personal and business matters connected with the death.

Isaac Todd, one of the co-executors of McTavish's will, wrote to John Askin to tell him about the fifty-four-year-old McTavish's death, saying that he had spent a lot of time with McTavish during his final days after returning from a trip to New York to find him very ill. After McTavish's death, Todd continued to visit his widow. As he put it, he was "the particular friend of his disconsolate wife [which] occasions my attention and many painful scenes."[1]

Another description of the circumstances of McTavish's death suggests that he died of pneumonia. "Full of health and spirits," McTavish had planned to build a magnificent new house. Work began on the mansion in the fall. In early spring, while supervising the work, he contracted a severe cold, "which being at first neglected soon became serious and past the power of medicine to treat."[2]

McTavish's death was difficult for McGillivray for a number of reasons. He was very close to his uncle and may have felt Simon's loss more than he did that of his father, who had died the previous year, because he had seen very little of his father since his first arrival in North America. Simon's death also meant that McGillivray would have to take over control of the NWC almost immediately. Finally, his task as chief executor of McTavish's will would not be an easy one. The estate was estimated to be worth £125,000, and McTavish left a young wife and four children under the age of eight. The will stated that the children were to be sent to England to be educated as soon as they were old enough, a condition to which their mother must agree. Apparently because of this requirement, she moved to England the following year.

The unfinished mansion was left to McTavish's seven-year-old son, William, and after him to succeeding male heirs. The land surrounding it was leased with the proviso that the lessee should maintain "in good order" the fence and railing enclosing the tomb of the late Simon McTavish.

On a trip to Britain shortly after his marriage, McTavish had paid a visit to the chief of Clan McTavish. When the chief secured the clan armorial bearings, Simon was granted the right to use them. After the chief died in 1796, leaving his family in financial difficulties, Simon gave the family generous financial assistance and arranged to bring the chief's son, John George McTavish, into the NWC as a clerk. John George became a partner in 1813 and a chief factor after the amalgamation of the NWC with the HBC.

McTavish also had purchased the ancestral clan seat of Dunardry in 1800. The terms of his will reflected the importance he attached to clan ties. He made elaborate provisions to keep Dunardry in the family and left legacies to a long list of relatives. Finally, the annual interest of one thousand pounds was to be used to assist "such of my poor relations in Scotland as I may have neglected to provide for by this my last will and testament."[3]

McTavish's love of splendour had led him to begin constructing a huge and very elaborate mansion. It was high enough on Mont Royal to be seen from all over the city and was built of limestone blocks rather than the rough fieldstones used for the houses built by many of his friends. At the time of his death, the house's roof was in place, but little work had been done in the interior. McTavish's executors decided to neither complete construction of the building nor demolish it. They merely filled the window openings with masonry, making the house resemble a larger version of the nearby mausoleum in which his body had been placed. A monument was erected over the mausoleum by William and Duncan McGillivray in 1806. McTavish's dream of building a mansion to be left to succeeding male heirs never came true. Not only was his magnificent home never completed, but none of his children lived to have children. Two died as infants; the other four died childless in their twenties.

Over the years, the house gradually deteriorated. Late in the nineteenth century someone wrote, "Thirty odd years ago there stood on the brow of Mount Royal a huge mansion, weather beaten, unfinished . . . It had been there since the memory of the oldest inhabitant, yet never had it changed its appearance . . . Three generations had known it under similar conditions . . . a relic of the ambitions of bygone days."[4] Not surprisingly, people soon began to say that the McTavish mansion was haunted. According to one story, McTavish had hung himself from its rafters. Another story said that "creatures not of this world" danced on the roof. This only happened when the moon was at a certain phase, causing it to gleam off the tin roof. Still other people claimed that McTavish was seen sliding down the hill in his coffin. The latter story could well be based in fact. A doctor on the McGill Faculty of Medicine lived in the area and resurrectionists, or body snatchers, supposedly delivered bodies to him from the pauper's graves in a nearby cemetery. The doctor then transported them by toboggan down the hill before delivering them to the hospital.[5]

Almost immediately following McTavish's death, the two North West Companies amalgamated. As Isaac Todd wrote:

There is a coalition . . . which will be to their interest and comfort
and be useful to society here. As far as my influence went with Mr.
McGillivray I promoted it. The New Company is to have one-
fourth of the whole but the business to be conducted by the old
and Sir Alexander Mackenzie is excluded from any interference.
With him and McGillivray there will, I fear, never be intimacy.[6]

The coalition agreement was signed on November 5, 1804, by the
partners of McTavish, Frobisher & Co. and twenty-three wintering partners for the NWC; signing for the XY Co. were two trading companies
and six wintering partners. The preamble to the agreement stated that
the two companies were "desirous to put an end to said opposition and
to avoid the waste of property attending thereon and to carry on the
said trade in a more advantageous manner." Mackenzie reorganized the
quarter interest that the XY Co. received into a unit under the name "Sir
Alexander Mackenzie and Company."[7]

It took McGillivray two years to complete the delicate task of reorganizing McTavish, Frobisher & Co., necessitated by the death of McTavish.
On December 1, 1806, he announced the formation of the new concern
that he named McTavish, McGillivrays & Co. The partners of the new
company were the McGillivray brothers, their brother-in-law Angus Shaw,
and the Hallowell brothers, James and William. William McGillivray
now presided over the largest business concern in British North America.
He also brought his youngest brother, Simon, into McTavish & Fraser at
this time. Unlike William and Duncan, who became NWC apprentices,
Simon spent much of his time in London because of a lame foot.

≡:≡

OVER THE WINTER of 1805–06, an American military man named
Lieutenant Zebulon Pike found that British merchandise traded at Fond
du Lac had not gone through American customs at Michilimackinac as
required. This angered Pike, and he was perhaps even more upset that the
British flag flew over several NWC posts and Native villages in the United
States. Pike ordered the Union Jack shot down from the flagpole at the
NWC post at Leech Lake.

At least partially in response to this hostile action, the NWC and
some other Montreal businessmen formed a partnership called the

Michilimackinac Company in 1806. The intention was to draw a line between the fur trade on the American side of the border—that is, south and west of Michilimackinac—and the North West trade and to co-operate to prevent competition between the two factions for a term of ten years. It was also hoped that this partnership would prevent any further incidents like the one involving Lieutenant Pike. Some winterers who were personally involved with the southwest trade, however, charged that McGillivray had overstepped his power of attorney in setting up the Michilimackinac Company. Daniel McKenzie called those who backed the Michilimackinac agreement "McGillivray's geese."[8]

After McTavish's death, Duncan McGillivray went to London to make yet another attempt to negotiate access to Hudson Bay. The minutes of the 1805 rendezvous state that the HBC was not disposed to grant such access without receiving what they considered sufficient payment from the NWC. The agents authorized McGillivray to offer the HBC a sum not exceeding two thousand pounds sterling per year. It was almost a year later before the HBC responded to this offer—the answer was no.

Another item dealt with at the 1805 meeting was marriage. All the partners agreed that the number of women and children to be supported in "Indian country" had become a burden and that a remedy must be found "to check so great an evil if nothing effectual could be done to suppress it entirely." The result was a rule stating that Nor'Westers were no longer allowed to marry First Nations women but that marriage to "the daughter of a white man after the fashion of the country should be considered no violation of this resolve." The penalty for disobeying this rule was a fine of one hundred pounds Halifax currency.[9]

At the 1807 rendezvous, the new NWC headquarters were renamed Fort William in honour of McGillivray. Trader Daniel Harmon, who was in attendance, wrote, "This which formerly was called the New Fort is now named Fort William . . . on which occasion the [company] made a present to their common labouring men of a considerable quantity of spirits and shrub and etc. and also a similar present was made to the Natives who are encamped about the Fort."[10]

In the summer of 1808, William McGillivray's seventeen-year-old twin sons, Joseph and Simon, were enrolled as apprentice clerks in the NWC. Joseph was among the thousand or more men at Fort William for that year's rendezvous. According to the 1808 rendezvous minutes, two men who had broken the law regarding marriage to Native women were fined.[11]

The enforcement of the terms of voyageur contracts was another issue dealt with in 1808. The bourgeois sometimes turned to courts of law to prosecute voyageurs who didn't fulfill their contracts, but other means of enforcement were usually sought because of the difficulty of apprehending and transporting delinquent voyageurs back to Montreal. In 1808, William McGillivray wrote to Forsyth, Ogilvy and McKenzie:

I agree with you that protecting deserters would be a dangerous practice and very pernicious to the trade and fully sensible of this when any man belonging to people opposed to the NWC have happened to come into our forts, we have told the master of such to come for them.[12]

When the NWC had allowed one of their engagés to return to Montreal due to ill health, they unsuccessfully attempted to arrest him when he afterward engaged to work for another company. McGillivray then requested that said company return the man or pay his debt. Whether or not McGillivray was successful in this instance is not known. Finally, however, he decided that if he wished to hire someone who was already under contract to another employer, it was easier to purchase that man's contract from his previous master. He warned other companies against hiring deserters and obviously hoped that they would follow the same procedure if a NWC deserter applied for work with them.[13]

The new NWC headquarters and annual rendezvous site, Fort William, reflected the company's prosperity and influence. Visitors to the fort were amazed at its size and the assortment of merchandise available there. The main square contained eleven buildings. Six of these buildings were stores that contained wholesale goods, while another building contained three retail outlets. There was also a large warehouse with two smaller buildings behind it where incoming furs were taken to be cleaned and packed into bales to be shipped to Montreal.

The dining room held two hundred people and was decorated with artwork. The art included a bust of Simon McTavish, portraits of the various proprietors, David Thompson's famous map, and two paintings presented by McGillivray—one representing the Battle of the Nile and the other a portrait of British admiral Horatio Nelson. A maître d' supervised kitchen and serving staff from Montreal who prepared and served the food and drink served at the gala banquets and dances held at each rendezvous.

Outside the fort walls were a shipyard in which the company's vessels were built and repaired, a kitchen garden, and a farm. One visitor wrote, "An observatory (rather a crazy structure) stands in the court yard . . . From it the eye takes in an extensive view of flat country, thickly wooded, with the bold shores of Thunder Island at a distance, rising abruptly out of Lake Superior." Immediately around the fort "the scene was enlivened by . . . groups of women, soldiers, voyageurs, and Indians, dancing, singing, drinking and gambling."[14]

American author Washington Irving wrote what might be considered a somewhat overblown description of a NWC rendezvous at Fort William. He said that in order to "behold the NWC in all its grandeur" it was necessary to witness the annual rendezvous. He likened the wintering partners to the chieftains of Highland clans and declared that attending the Fort William rendezvous was as important to them as a meeting of Parliament was to the chieftains in Scotland. The partners from Montreal (the agents) travelled to the rendezvous in great state. They were wrapped in rich furs, with their huge canoes loaded with every convenience and luxury. In the council hall, "every member felt as if sitting in parliament, and every retainer and dependent looked up to the assemblage with awe as to the House of Lords . . . These grave and weighty councils were alternated by huge feasts and revels, like some of the old feasts described in Highland castles. The tables in the great banqueting room groaned under the weight of food."[15]

Irving also wrote about the agents and wintering partners who would appear in New York on business or for pleasure. There was "a degree of magnificence of purse about them, and a peculiar propensity to expenditure at the goldsmith's and jeweller's for rings, chains, brooches, necklaces, jewelled watches, and other rich trinkets" both for themselves and as gifts to their female acquaintances.[16]

—※—

UNLIKE HIS BROTHER William, who was delighted to leave le pays d'en haut and live in Montreal, Duncan McGillivray was anxious to make his mark as an explorer. In 1800, he was sent, along with David Thompson and five other men, to search for the Columbia River (also known as the Great River of the West). In late November, the group arrived at the site where Calgary is now located, but could go no farther without a guide. As a result, they returned to Rocky Mountain House for the winter. There, Duncan took sick, possibly with rheumatic fever, and by spring he was so ill that he had to return to Montreal on crutches. Although he lived for another seven years and continued to work in the fur trade, Duncan never completely recovered his health and was unable to return to the active exploration that he preferred.

On March 10, 1808, William McGillivray wrote to Mr. Justice Reid (husband of his sister Betsy), "I cannot communicate to you any pleasing intelligence of Duncan's health. I consider him this last week as losing ground, and altho' I have every hope from the effects of the warm spring on him I must confess that I live . . . with some degree of dread."[17]

Duncan died on April 9, 1808. He had argued earlier that year that a trade monopoly was good for British interests. The chief benefit of a single company, he said, was that it rendered the Indians "dependent; and consequently industrious and subordinate; and being subordinate they are preserved faithful to the Government." As a result, they would, at the request of the government, "at any moment abandon the chase and take up the hatchet." In other words, they would go to war for the British if asked to do so.[18]

Although there is no record of Duncan ever marrying, he made provision in his will for a daughter named Magdalen. She was baptized at Christ Church in Montreal with William's wife as her godmother. Nothing is known of the child's mother; she may have been dead or perhaps merely no longer had any connection with Duncan. It is also unknown who the child's guardians were, where she lived, or what happened to her in later life.[19]

During the first decade of the nineteenth century William McGillivray not only lost his brother and uncle but also suffered tragedy in his own household. Magdalen gave birth to six children, but only two of them—daughters born in May 1805 and March 1808—lived for more than a few months. McGillivray wrote to his sister Betsy on March 17, 1808, "I have the pleasure of announcing to you the birth of a daughter . . . The mother and she are both doing well; this event happened at 8 o'clock this morning."[20]

The Fur Traders at Montreal, pastel painting by George Agnew Reid, 1916. The annual fur fair was organized by the government of New France to discourage Native trappers from trading with coureurs du bois (unlicensed traders). LIBRARY AND ARCHIVES CANADA, ACCESSION NO. 1990-329-1, C-011013

The 1871 painting *Voyageurs at Dawn*, by Frances Anne Hopkins, 1871, portrays members of a fur-trade brigade. LIBRARY AND ARCHIVES CANADA, ACCESSION NO. 1989-401-3, C-002773

North View of Montreal showing the old fortifications, ca. 1793, taken from Joseph Frobisher's country house, Beaver Hall. Painting by George Elliot. LIBRARY AND ARCHIVES CANADA, ACCESSION NO. 1989-470-5R, C-012755

Duncan McGillivray's Beaver Club medal. McCORD MUSEUM M20988 10

Simon McTavish, portrayed ca. 1800, headed the North West Company until his death in 1804.

William and Magdalen McGillivray, their daughter Anne, and pets in an 1806 portrait by
William Berczy. McCORD MUSEUM M18683

This painting titled *Montreal from the Mountain*, by James Duncan, shows Château St. Antoine, the McGillivray country estate. McCORD MUSEUM M966.61-P2

This portrait of a man in Highland dress was long thought to be of William McGillivray; however, it is now thought more likely to represent his brother Duncan. FORT WILLIAM HISTORICAL PARK

A portrait of John McDonald of Garth, NWC partner and brother of Magdalen McGillivray, painted by Donald Hill. McCORD MUSEUM M1594

Simon McGillivray was painted wearing his Masonic regalia, ca. 1824, by Richard Reinagle.

This baby, born just a few weeks before the death of her uncle Duncan, was named Magdalen Julia. The birth of the McGillivrays' only son, who died at the age of seven months, took place in August 1809.

In 1800, McGillivray purchased a piece of land in the Montreal suburb of St. Antoine. It was a beautiful site, crossed by a stream and backed by Mont Royal. The St. Lawrence flowed to the south of the property. In the summer of 1802, McGillivray began construction of a Georgian-style home there, along with stables, an icehouse, and a carriage house. The family moved into the new house, which they named Château St. Antoine, in the summer of 1805. McGillivray also bought a second farm where he built a private park with formal gardens and an ornamental pond.

Soon every visitor of note to Montreal and all the McGillivray relatives and friends were being entertained in the spacious Château St. Antoine. James McGill and Joseph Frobisher were neighbours, and Frobisher frequently wrote in his diary about visiting with the McGillivray family. On December 22, 1809, he wrote, "Dined McG. anniversary of their marriage. 9 years." On March 7, 1810, "Mr. McGillivray's child was buried in the family vault at the mountain," And on May 19, "Dined with Mr. McGillivray, Anne's birthday. 5 years old."[21]

On May 21, a family friend wrote to another acquaintance, "Mr. McGillivray is at present much distressed at Mrs. McGillivray's situation, which has become so serious as to have called for the opinion of Dr. Selby that a voyage to England is indispensable to give a chance for the re-establishment of her health. I fear she is far gone in a decline."[22]

Frobisher wrote another series of anxious entries in his diary from late June 1810 until late July. He mentioned seeing the McGillivray family off for Quebec and that Magdalen sailed from there to England on July 6. On July 24, he wrote that he met General Brock at McGillivray's house, and on July 31, he commented that it was twenty-six days since Mrs. McGillivray sailed from Quebec. She and the children were travelling in the care of Isaac Todd and his daughter. About six weeks after the July 31 entry, Frobisher died at the age of 70.

Magdalen went to London, where she stayed with relatives. McGillivray spent a month negotiating with John Jacob Astor in New York before he finally felt able to leave for England in the late fall. He never saw his wife again, as she died in the first week of January 1811, and he did not arrive in London until the end of February.

Alexander Henry the Elder wrote to John Askin on February 10, 1811, mentioning the deaths of many friends—the wife of Commodore Grant, Joseph Frobisher, and Mrs. McGillivray. He commented that in the last two years Montreal had greatly changed with many new inhabitants, mostly American merchants, doubling the population. "There is but little French spoken here at present . . . I am grown so old that it is a difficult matter with me to make new acquaintances as my old ones are all dead." Both Askin and Henry were seventy-one at the time, and Todd was sixty-eight. "Todd was once much older than me, but he has grown much younger at present," Henry quipped.[23]

By early 1811, McGillivray must have felt that he had faced more than his share of personal loss over the previous dozen years—the end of his close friendship with Alexander Mackenzie followed by the deaths of his uncle Simon, his brother Duncan, four infant children, and his wife Magdalen. He could not then have imagined the new problems that would soon face him as head of the NWC.

10 THE NORTH WEST COMPANY, LORD SELKIRK, AND THE WAR OF 1812, 1811—14

Upon the shores of Hudson's Bay,
Where Arctic winters, stern and grey,
Freeze the salt-waters of the Deep
In a long, silent icy sleep;
Where willows and the stunted pine
Can scarcely live in such a clime,
Where Arctic fox and polar bear,
Clad in a coat of snow-white hair,
Prowl forth to snuff the tainted gale
And feast on walrus or the whale;
With snow and ice encompassed round,
And built on low and swampy ground,
Through which Haye's River takes its way
And slowly joins the frozen Bay;
There in its cold and icy lands,
Silent and grim, York Factory stands.

FROM AN UNPUBLISHED POEM BY
HBC CLERK R.M. BALLANTYNE[1]

The following advertisement appeared in the *Inverness Journal* on April 19, 1811:

> Wanted, *a few young, active, stout men for the service of the Hudson's Bay Company, at their factories and settlements in America . . . The Company have resolved to encourage a settlement in a pair of their territories, which enjoys a good climate, and favourable soil and situation; and those of their servants as renew their contracts for two years, will have their wages augmented, and an additional hundred acres granted them. In the country where the Company are forming their new settlement, there are several fine rivers running through fertile lands [with] the climate same as at Montreal, Canada, Nova Scotia, or Prince Edward's Island. Wheat, oats, barley, India corn, potatoes, hemp, flax and tobacco will thrive in it.*

Thomas Douglas, the Earl of Selkirk, was the Scottish nobleman responsible for placing this advertisement. When Simon McGillivray responded to Selkirk's advertisement anonymously on behalf of the NWC, it was the opening salvo in a war of words between the Nor'Westers and the supporters of Selkirk and the HBC, waged in letters to the editor published in the *Inverness Journal*.

Under the signature "A Highlander," Simon claimed that a considerable number of people had been engaged not only as HBC servants but also to go as settlers immediately. He warned these people "of the dangers and disasters which they are ignorantly going to encounter." He charged that many points made in the advertisement were false, or at least misleading, and pointed out that, as yet, there were no settlements, although the advertisement spoke as if settlements already existed. Secondly, the settlement would be so far inland from Hudson Bay that it would take settlers almost a year to complete the trip from Scotland. As a result, they would have to pass their first winter at York Factory. There, many would perish from excessive cold and want of food if a sufficient supply of provisions was not shipped with them *"for they will find none in the country"* (italics in original). Finally, the settlement would be surrounded by warlike nations who would consider the settlers as intruders and thus destroy their homes, crops, and livestock.

Thomas Douglas, 5th Earl of Selkirk, brought Scottish settlers to colonize the Red River area.

"A Highlander" concluded by saying that if all the people now assembling in response to the advertisement "were engaged *bona fide* for the service of the HBC" he would not have thought it necessary to write this letter because it is true that "Company servants are always well treated. They receive good wages and food and . . . the Company *always engages to carry them back to Scotland at the end of their service.*"[2]

The next round in the war of words was a letter from an HBC chaplain, refuting "A Highlander's" claims. Two weeks later "A Highlander" responded with a letter saying that some of the emigrants "who had been decoyed on board [ship] on a promise of being furnished with a cabin passage and of messing at the captain's table—being on the contrary thrust into the hold and fed upon oatmeal and water, mutinied, jumped overboard and attempted to make their escape."[3]

Almost a year after the original ad was published, sworn statements by the master and second mate of the ship in question were published refuting the above charges. They stated that no emigrants were intended to sail on board these ships which left in 1811. The men whom "A Highlander" represented as emigrants were actually *servants*, "who were attempting to violate their own voluntary contracts and to defraud their employers of the money which they had received in part as wages." The only concession to "A Highlander's" charges that the captain was willing to make was to question if the HBC agents "in the performance of this duty . . . did not exceed the due bounds of temper and moderation."[4]

On May 22, 1812, someone who signed his name as A.B. wrote in support of the HBC, saying that it would be a benefit to the NWC if the HBC could be prevented from obtaining sufficient men to conduct their business. A.B. charged that many copies of the *Inverness Journal* were distributed free of charge to people in the Orkneys and Stornoway who normally did not take the paper. Then A.B. asked two questions: Who paid for these newspapers and ordered them distributed, and were "The Highlander" and Simon McGillivray one and the same person? Obviously A.B. was convinced that he knew the answers to these questions: The NWC had circulated the newspapers, and McGillivray was indeed "A Highlander."[5]

Selkirk, becoming aware of the strength of opposition to his plans for a settlement at the Red River, asked British MP Sir James Montgomery for assistance. Montgomery wrote to the office of the British Admiralty, which responded negatively. "We cannot grant the protection which Lord Selkirk desires for the passengers on board the [ship] *Robert Taylor*; if they are landsmen and not liable to the impress [for naval duty], they require no protection. If any of them are liable it will be the duty of the naval officers to detain them for the King's service."[6] The impress referred to by the British Admiralty was for service in the War of 1812.

Selkirk had been interested in resettling Highlanders in North America for at least a decade. When he had visited Montreal in 1803, he was lavishly feted at the Beaver Club; however, William McGillivray had distrusted him. He felt that Selkirk asked too many questions and it was known that he had an interest in the HBC. At the time, Alexander Mackenzie had suggested that for twenty thousand pounds the NWC could buy up a controlling share of the HBC, but McGillivray had opposed that idea since the HBC was having financial difficulties.

Five years later, the HBC Committee minutes of November 16, 1808, stated that HBC stocks worth £800 had been transferred to Alexander Mackenzie and £742 to the Earl of Selkirk. By 1810, Selkirk personally controlled almost half of the shares in the HBC. For all practical purposes, Selkirk, his wife, and her relatives had control over the company. Mackenzie was furious when he learned that Selkirk had gained control so he could establish a settlement rather than further the fur trade. The two men quarrelled violently. Mackenzie turned his stocks over to McGillivray and urged Nor'Westers to buy up what stocks they could on the open market; however, by that time it was too late for the NWC to have any chance to prevent Selkirk's actions.

According to Selkirk, a man named Edward Ellice tried to intimidate him by warning that the NWC wintering partners would stop at nothing to destroy his colony. Selkirk claimed that Ellice wrote that the partners were a group of men "utterly destitute of all moral principle or the feelings of honour prevalent in civilized society," that they were generally of the lowest social level and selected from among the indigent relatives of the leading partners, and that they would be willing to "commit any crime which was necessary to effect the views of their associates in the concern." Selkirk retorted that "he had not previously heard so correct a description of the North West Company," and carried on with his plans.[7] There are, however, reasons to doubt Selkirk's claim. Ellice continued to work with the Nor'Westers over the next decade, and it seems unlikely that he could have made such a statement without the story getting back to the Nor'Westers and utterly destroying his business relationship with them.

The Nor'Westers were not the only ones opposed to Selkirk's proposed settlement. Many HBC men were also against it and plainly admitted that only the high cost of imported provisions and the difficulty of recruiting servants led them to reluctantly agree to the founding of the colony.

On May 25, 1811, Simon McGillivray wrote a letter to William describing Selkirk's plans. He said that Selkirk had concluded an agreement with the HBC to give him "a grant in perpetuity of the whole country on the Red River" in which to settle colonists. In exchange, Selkirk was to provide two hundred men annually to work for the

HBC, "and after his settlement is founded to supply them with certain quantities of provisions."[8]

The following spring, Simon wrote twice about Selkirk to the wintering partners. In his first letter, he told them that Selkirk's colony would cause much expense to the NWC before he was driven to abandon the project; "yet he must be driven to abandon it, for his success would strike at the very existence of our trade."[9]

Simon sent a second letter to be read at the 1812 Fort William rendezvous. In it, he requested an account of the arrival of the first party of settlers at the Red River. "If you can transmit to me a narrative of their proceedings and sufferings, authenticated if possible by affidavit, it will answer an excellent purpose [as material for further letters from] A Highlander."[10]

The proposed settlement at the Red River was not the only cause for concern at the 1812 rendezvous. The wintering partners learned that the War of 1812 had been declared when NWC partner William McKay appeared via express canoe with the news. McKay had left Quebec on June 25 with orders from Governor General George Prévost to be delivered to the British garrison at St. Joseph's Island and the NWC at Fort William. Both establishments were to send expeditions immediately to Michilimackinac and take it by surprise. By the time the men from Fort William reached Michilimackinac, volunteers from St. Joseph's Island had seized it without firing a shot, and the British were able to hold on to it until the war ended.

Donald McTavish and John McDonald of Garth were dispatched to London to arrange British naval support for the NWC ship *Isaac Todd*, which would be sent armed from the British Isles to the Pacific coast (see Chapter 14 for an account of the NWC's Pacific trade). Other Nor'Westers were ordered overland to meet *Isaac Todd*. In the spring of 1813, McTavish and McDonald successfully obtained naval support when Captain James Hillyar of HMS *Phoebe* received secret orders to escort *Isaac Todd* to the Columbia River. Captain Hillyar was told "to protect and render every assistance in your power to British traders from Canada and to destroy, and if possible totally annihilate, any settlements which the Americans may have formed on the Columbia River."[11]

The heads of both the NWC and the South West (Michilimackinac) Fur Company had written to British military officials before war broke out to say that they would "enter with zeal into any measures of defence, *or even offence* that may be proposed to them." The traders suggested that they could combine their defences with the regular troops. If the enemy became established upon any point in Lake Huron, the traders would arm one of their vessels and carry with them every man they could muster, amounting to about three hundred voyageurs and as many Natives. This force, along with any available regular force from York, "would enable them to . . . exclude [the enemy] from any navigation or commerce of Lakes Superior, Huron and Michigan."[12]

William McGillivray had a reputation as being very knowledgeable about supplies, transport, and dealing with Native peoples on both sides of the still ill-defined border. As a result, he was frequently consulted by both British officials and John Jacob Astor during the war. Astor wanted help in getting British goods to the American Indians. By the spring of 1812, Astor was trying to get Congress to waive the Non-Importation Act for him so that he could import his share of the trade goods stored at St. Joseph Island. He also tried more devious means, playing one country off against the other. In June, Astor asked his Montreal partners to ignore the embargo. They refused, saying that the goods had been imported for the joint use of the South West Fur Company and the NWC, and "as Mr. McGillivray, who has a very material agency in that agreement is absent," the goods would remain on the British side of the border at St. Joseph's Island.[13]

It seems possible that McGillivray was not far from St. Joseph's Island at the time. The island was the crossroads of east-west travel, where large supplies of arms, ammunition, and liquor were stored. It was also close to Sault Ste. Marie, a strategic NWC site that guarded access to Lake Superior and contained extensive stores of corn and other provisions.

In October 1812, the NWC offered the services of its engagés for wartime service, and the Corps of Canadian Voyageurs was created under the command of William McGillivray. The Corps was designed to militarize the voyageurs who were essential for moving supplies to the North West and responsible for maintaining the fur trade during the war. It consisted of a captain, ten lieutenants, and ten conductors (sergeants) promoted from among the voyageurs, in addition to some four hundred voyageurs with the rank of private. The men were equipped with rifles, small axes, and knives; but they refused to wear standard military uniforms, claiming that the red coats were unsuitable for paddling. The Crown also issued each man a sword, a pike, and a pistol, but most either sold or discarded these items. Although undisciplined, the voyageurs proved valuable to the British war effort. Nevertheless, the British replaced them with the army commissariat in March 1813 because they thought "a more formal and regimented unit" would be more suitable for handling military resupply duties.[14]

In recognition of his war efforts, McGillivray was appointed to the Legislative Council of Lower Canada on January 25, 1813, receiving the title Honourable Lieutenant-Colonel William McGillivray. Although the Governor General ordered the Corps of Voyageurs disbanded six months after its formation, he did praise them for "their zealous and disinterested service."[15]

William's son, Lieutenant Joseph McGillivray, wrote a vivid description of the members of the Corps of Canadian Voyageurs. "In moments when danger ought to have produced a little steadiness, they completely set discipline at defiance, and . . . broke out into all the unrestrained mirth and anti-military familiarity of the thoughtless voyageur . . . Notwithstanding these peculiarities, the voyageurs were excellent partisans, and from their superior knowledge of the country, were able to render material service during the war."[16]

The voyageurs generally came on parade with pipes in their mouths and their rations of pork and bread stuck on their bayonets. On seeing an officer, they would take off their hats and make a low bow and greet him with "Bon jour, Monsieur le Général" (or whatever rank applied). If they knew the officer was married, they would also inquire after the health of "Madame et les enfants." On parade they talked incessantly, and when called to order and told to be quiet, they would reply that the commanding officer should let them off as quickly as possible because they had not yet had breakfast or it was almost an hour since they had last had a smoke. Repeated infractions of military discipline meant that many voyageurs were temporarily imprisoned. However, if the man on overnight guard duty was a voyageur, he would often tell the prisoners "aller coucher avec sa femme, et retourner le lendemain de bonne heure." They would obey that order, returning early in the morning as promised. The voyageurs had great confidence in their officers, especially Colonel McGillivray, whose influence frequently saved them from punishment.[17]

After the death of General Brock at the Battle of Queenston Heights, McGillivray was made an honorary aide-de-camp to Governor General Sir George Prévost. When an attack on Montreal seemed imminent, McGillivray offered his services to the local commandant and suggested that most of the Natives in the area would be willing to serve in the Corps of Canadian Voyageurs. "They are troublesome colleagues 'tis true, but, in these times this must be overlooked. I think they would be of more use with us [than under regular military command]."[18]

By the end of 1813, the Americans were in control of Lake Erie. Colonel McDougall, the officer in charge of the western posts, wrote to ask McGillivray (who had been ill) if he would be able to supply Michilimackinac in the event of an American attack. McDougall also referred to a proposal made earlier by McGillivray to build some gunboats. Prévost, according to McDougall, was "ready to sanction at any expense and to man with seamen" these boats, providing that McGillivray would "undertake to find a sufficient number of carpenters of respectability and enterprise" to build them. Prévost was also willing to employ some of "your voyageurs . . . a measure that will be highly useful, and backed with your powerful influence, not very difficult to accomplish."[19]

The declaration of the War of 1812 had demonstrated the superiority of the NWC communications system over that of the Americans. A man connected with the NWC happened to be in Washington when war was declared and immediately dispatched messages by express through chains of correspondents to two places in the Canadas. NWC agents then forwarded the information to the government at Quebec City, where it arrived in within six days from Washington. This is in stark contrast to the slow movement of communications generally in North America at that time, where it took two weeks for one American general to learn that he was at war.[20]

In 1815, William McKay, a veteran trader and NWC partner, wrote an account of his activities during the War of 1812. McKay was one of the first to volunteer his services to defend the country. General Prévost accepted his offer and ordered him to carry a dispatch from Quebec on June 25 to the commander at St. Joseph's Island, telling him that war had been declared. The trip took McKay eight days. The dispatch stated in part:

I am commanded to acquaint you that . . . the American Government has declared war against Great Britain . . . The gentlemen of the NWC have assured the commander of the forces [Prévost] of their cordial and active co-operation in aiding the exertions of H.M. Government by every means in their power, and I am commanded to inform you that it is His Excellency's most express orders that you will to the utmost of your ability afford every assistance and protection possible to promote the interest and security of the NWC. Mr. McKay, the bearer of this is a proprietor of the NWC.[21]

Immediately following his trip to St. Joseph's Island, McKay travelled three thousand miles over thirty-two days to secure all the arms and ammunition, provisions, and ships that the NWC could provide to the war effort. McKay's next task involved raising the Corps of Canadian Voyageurs. McKay makes two contradictory statements about the disbanding of the corps. In one he says that it was disbanded in the spring of 1813, only a few months after it came into existence, but he also states that following the war the various embodied (volunteer) militia, including the Corps of Canadian Voyageurs, were disbanded by an order issued on March 1, 1815. According to that account, the voyageurs who had been enrolled as members of the corps would have received pay until March 24, 1815, even if they were not on active duty.[22]

In July 1814, American forces attacked the NWC depot at Sault Ste. Marie. Gabriel Franchère, a former employee of Astor's Pacific Fur Company, was travelling home to Montreal and left Fort William in McDonald of Garth's express canoe on July 20. A few days later, they met a canoe carrying Captain Robert McCargo and the crew of the NWC schooner *Perseverance*. McCargo told the McDonald party that he had narrowly escaped the Americans who had raided the Sault and that he had scuttled his fully laden ship to prevent them from capturing it. As a result, McDonald and McCargo decided to return to Fort William to warn the other partners who were still at the rendezvous. Franchère and several others continued east in McCargo's canoe.

Franchère's group learned more details about what had happened at the Sault a couple of days later. About 150 Americans had stolen everything of value and then burned the village, although they did not harm any of the inhabitants. On July 30, McDonald and William McGillivray caught up to Franchère. The next day, they proceeded to the Sault where the NWC buildings were still smoking. On August 1, they tried to send a courier to Michilimackinac to inform the commandant there what had happened; however, Michilimackinac was completely blockaded. As a result, the party of forty-seven NWC canoes continued eastward, laden with furs and manned by 325 well-armed men. The Nor'Westers safely reached Montreal with their cargo on September 1.

The Treaty of Ghent ended the war in December 1814. It decreed the return of all captured territories to their previous owners. This left the ownership of Fort Astoria on the Pacific coast in dispute. Did it belong to the NWC by right of purchase or had it been captured by them from the Americans as a prize of war? When John McDonald of Garth had reached the mouth of the Columbia in the fall of 1813, he had learned that Fort Astoria and the Pacific Fur Company had been taken over by Nor'Westers led by John George McTavish because the Americans were short of provisions and feared that a British warship was coming to attack them. McDonald ceremoniously took over Fort Astoria. The Stars and Stripes was lowered, the Union Jack was raised, and the name of Astoria was changed to Fort George.[23]

The "unfortunate cession of the fort and island of Michilimackinac to the United States" also raised "strong apprehensions" among Nor'Westers about the security of the international boundary.[24] McGillivray told General Prévost that the friendship of Natives in American territory must be preserved, both for the sake of the fur trade and for the safety of Upper Canada. To that end, McGillivray urged a strong military presence near Michilimackinac. While neither the Americans nor the British can be said to have won the war, it was a certainly a setback for the Nor'Westers. Not only did the NWC suffer severe property losses, it also lost its last chance to control the American "Old Northwest" between Lakes Huron and Michigan and south and west of Lake Superior.

11 THE ARRIVAL OF THE RED RIVER SETTLERS, 1812—14

There was trouble at the rendezvous
When the governor seized the buffalo meat
from the stores at La Souris,
The Nor'Westers vowed a sweet revenge.
Commissions were renewed
For McGillivray and the disbanded
Corps of Canadians Voyageurs
Where the Red River meets the Assiniboine
in the King's name they did forge
When the governor seized the buffalo meat
he started the Pemmican War.

RODNEY BROWN, FROM "PEMMICAN WAR"[1]

In late August 1812, Miles MacDonnell, who had been appointed governor of Selkirk's Red River settlement, arrived at the proposed site of the settlement with the first group of settlers. He camped along the Red River across from the NWC's Fort Gibraltar. Five days later, MacDonnell formally read the patent of the land grant given to Selkirk, which was to be known as Assiniboia. One of the Nor'Westers in the small crowd that turned out for the ceremony was Alexander

MacDonnell of Greenfield, who was both Governor MacDonnell's first cousin and his brother-in-law. After the conclusion of the business, the governor invited the gentlemen to meet at his tent for a drink, and a keg of spirits was turned out for the "common" people."[2]

Initially, the relationship between Governor MacDonnell and the Nor'Westers was cordial. The governor wrote in his diary that shortly after their arrival the Nor'Westers invited him and HBC officer William Hillier to dinner. "We passed a very pleasant evening and only returned at 1 AM"[3]

Because the buffalo herds were closer to Pembina than The Forks, the settlers were taken to spend the winter at Pembina, and buffalo hunters were hired to provide them with meat. MacDonnell of Greenfield was the chief NWC trader at Pembina over the winter of 1812–13. By the spring, Governor MacDonnell was accusing his cousin Greenfield and the other Nor'Westers of "insidious and treacherous conduct during the winter in endeavouring to swerve my people from their duty." He wrote to Selkirk in July 17, "I have been interfered with and opposed on all sides. The NWC tampered with my people . . . even some in the employ of the HBC acted with more hostility than friendship. My situation all last winter was uncomfortable in the extreme."[4]

One of the settlers deserted to the NWC over the winter. The Nor'Westers took him to Fort William in the spring of 1813, but he was sent back to the Red River because, at that point, the partners of the NWC "did not think it prudent" to openly war against the settlement.[5] This somewhat cautious attitude soon changed when Governor MacDonnell took action that virtually guaranteed that the Nor'Westers would commence open hostility against the settlement. On January 8, 1814, he issued the infamous "Pemmican Proclamation." The preamble of the proclamation stated that the welfare of the settlers made it essential to provide enough food for them. As a result, for a period of one year, no traders within Selkirk's territory should take any provisions out of the territory except for those necessary to carry trading parties presently in the territory to their respective destinations. To add insult to injury in the eyes of the Nor'Westers, the NWC had to apply to MacDonnell for a licence to remove these necessary provisions.[6]

In the view of the NWC, the proclamation not only placed their food supply under the control of the HBC, it also asserted the authority of the governor over the whole Red River country. Selkirk and the HBC believed that such authority was derived from the HBC charter of 1670. The Nor'Westers, on the other hand, claimed that the Red River country had been French Canadian by right of French exploration and occupation previous to the Treaty of Paris in 1763, at which time it passed (with Canada) to the British Crown. The NWC pointed to the Canada Jurisdiction Act of 1803, by which crimes committed in "Indian country" were to be tried in Canadian courts, as proof of this.

In the winter of 1813–14, NWC trader John Pritchard was ordered to buy up as many provisions as he possibly could. In the spring, he brought these provisions to the Souris River post from the Qu'Appelle River. It was not until he arrived at Souris that he learned about the Pemmican Proclamation. Pritchard was ordered to remain at Souris with the provisions, awaiting further orders. Shortly afterward, Sheriff John Spencer arrived at Fort Souris with Governor MacDonnell's warrant to seize the provisions. When Pritchard refused to open the fort's gate, Spencer ordered his men to force their way in and to break down the door of the storehouse with hatchets. They seized six hundred sacks of pemmican and took them to the nearby HBC fort of Brandon House.

When John McDonald of Garth arrived at The Forks on his way to Fort William for the 1814 rendezvous, the situation at the settlement was extremely tense. Pritchard had just come from Souris and reported the attack there. His superior (likely Duncan Cameron) labelled him a coward for not defending the fort more vigorously. Governor MacDonnell found his 88 men opposed by 120 angry and excited Nor'Westers. The two sides, led by MacDonnell and McDonald of Garth respectively, managed to negotiate an agreement. As Pritchard described it, "Some papers of a conciliatory nature were written by me under the direction of the partners present . . . and signed by the parties."[7] Only Greenfield disagreed.

The NWC wintering partners rushed to Fort William by light canoe to discuss the settlement negotiated by McDonald of Garth on their behalf with the agents. William McGillivray was outraged. "It is the first time the North-West Company has ever been insulted," he stormed. He told John Pritchard that "he had acted like a coward" and censured McDonald of Garth for playing the peacemaker in negotiating the settlement. When Pritchard responded "that a different conduct would have led to bloodshed, McGillivray replied with a sneer that he knew better, adding that it was not the value of the provisions he regretted, but the insult offered to the concern."[8] As a result, Pritchard resigned from the NWC and told McGillivray that he was going to settle at the Red River. McGillivray responded that he "could not countenance" him there after what had happened and offered him land at York instead. Pritchard declined that offer, but he was advised by a fellow clerk "not to attempt returning to Red River Country contrary to the wishes of the Company or they would get me murdered on the road." As a result, Pritchard temporarily went to Montreal.[9]

Archibald Norman McLeod, second-in-command to McGillivray at Fort William, agreed with McGillivray regarding the embarrassment to the NWC. He wrote that "it will take years of active and persevering industry to do away the impression made by the unfortunate compromise of our honour at Red River."[10]

Greenfield and Duncan Cameron were given the job of repairing that compromised honour. Cameron was authorized to move as many settlers as possible to Upper Canada free of charge. He was also ordered to take Governor MacDonnell prisoner. Archibald Norman McLeod, as Justice of the Peace, supplied the winterers with warrants to make any arrests they felt were necessary.

Although the NWC agents always maintained that they never ordered Greenfield and Cameron to mount a campaign against the settlement, a letter written by Greenfield to John McDonald of Garth on August 5, 1814, suggests otherwise:

> *You see myself and our mutual friend Cameron so far on our way to commence open hostilities against the enemy in Red River; much is expected from us . . . One thing certain [is] that we will do our best to defend what we consider our rights in the interior. Something serious will undoubtedly take place. Nothing but the complete downfall of the colony will satisfy some by fair or foul means. A most desirable object, if it can be accomplished; so here is at them with all my heart and energy.*[11]

Greenfield and Cameron arrived at the Red River in August 1814 dressed in military uniforms. Cameron—resplendent in a major's uniform that had belonged to Archibald Norman McLeod during the War of 1812—told the settlers that he was a captain and Greenfield was a lieutenant in the Corps of Canadian Voyageurs at the Red River. Not only that, Cameron also stated that he was "chief of the country" rather than Miles MacDonnell, and that William McGillivray had the rank of Lieutenant-Colonel.[12] Cameron and Greenfield showed the settlers their commissions, signed by the commandant at Michilimackinac.

When Selkirk learned what had happened, he complained to Sir Gordon Drummond, who was in charge of the military in Canada. Drummond refused to take any action, replying that because the public had already been informed of the "discharge of the late Corps of Canadian Voyageurs, any further declaration on the part of the provincial government relating to that corps must be deemed unnecessary."[13]

Greenfield left The Forks in the fall of 1814, but Cameron remained over the following winter, "during the whole of which period he did everything in his power to gain influence over the settlers."[14] He began inviting the heads of families to visit him and entertained them with dinners, balls, and large allowances of liquor. Cameron had the advantage of being able to talk to them in their native Gaelic, and he soon made them discontented with their situation and prospects. He told them that he would find them a free passage to Canada the following spring, where they would receive land. He also told them that if they did not leave, the Natives were determined to destroy the settlement. Only later did the settlers realize that, on the contrary, most of the Natives were actually trying to protect them.

In April 1815, Cameron, with about a dozen armed men, assisted the settlers in stealing artillery belonging to the settlement. After that, most of the settlers removed their families and all their effects to "Cameron's house"—likely meaning the NWC's Fort Gibraltar rather than Cameron's personal residence. In June, the Nor'Westers told the settlers that they only wanted to arrest Governor MacDonnell and promised to leave the settlement in peace if he was delivered up to them. After Governor MacDonnell was arrested and taken off to Canada, however, the NWC did not keep their promise to leave the settlers in peace, giving the excuse that they could not control the Métis, who had not promised to be bound by the agreement.

One hundred and forty settlers agreed to accompany Cameron to Fort William on their way to a promised better life in Upper Canada, but another sixty wished to remain in the settlement. On June 22, the governor's house was fired upon for about twenty minutes in the middle of the night. As a result, those settlers who had wished to stay at the settlement sent a letter the next day to Greenfield, promising to leave in a few days. Two Saulteaux chiefs and a group of warriors unsuccessfully tried to prevail upon the Nor'Westers to allow the settlers to remain. When that failed, the Saulteaux escorted the settlers down the river to Lake Winnipeg, and Cameron ordered the colony burned. The settlers crossed the lake to Jack River House where they remained for about a month before most of them returned to the settlement under the charge of Colin Robertson of the HBC. Jack River House became known as Norway House in 1817.

Although the Nor'Westers wanted to get rid of the settlers, many did not agree with the methods used by Cameron and Greenfield. In fact, Nor'Wester J.D. Cameron wrote, "Every neutral person thinks we are in the wrong by bringing out the colonists and destroying their houses."[15]

On the other hand, even people who were strong supporters of Selkirk blamed Governor MacDonnell for much of what had happened. One wrote that the governor had good administrative skills, but "he was inclined to be stubborn and arrogant" in his behaviour toward the Nor'Westers. In passing the Pemmican Proclamation, he committed an act that, though "legally right, was nothing less than foolhardy . . . [and] brought disaster in its train."[16]

Just a few months after issuing the Pemmican Proclamation in January 1814, Governor MacDonnell issued his second proclamation. It prohibited the running of buffalo on horseback because it drove them away from the settlement area and made it more difficult for the settlers (who had few horses) to hunt. This infuriated the Métis, who hunted buffalo on horseback and were very proud of their skills and those of their horses. The NWC fed this anger and pushed the idea that the Métis were in fact a new nation, a tribe with rights like those of their Native mothers. In order to strengthen Métis support, the NWC named four men—Cuthbert Grant, William Fraser, Angus Shaw, and Nicholas Montour—as "captains of the Métis" in the fall of 1814. All four men were sons of NWC partners. "With the eagerness of youth and the unquestioning loyalty of the clansman," these men made their bourgeois's cause their own.[17]

Brothers Robert and Cuthbert Grant—the uncle and father of the Métis captain appointed by the NWC—were Scottish-born wintering partners. William McGillivray had spent his first year in the North West working under Robert. Although there is no record of any connection between Cuthbert Grant and McGillivray, a relationship must have existed since McGillivray was named as executor of Cuthbert's will and guardian to his son Cuthbert Jr. In June 1801, when Cuthbert Jr. was eight, he travelled from his prairie home to Grand Portage with the brigade. From there, McGillivray took him to Montreal where he was baptized at the St. Gabriel Street Presbyterian Church with McGillivray and Roderick McKenzie as his godfathers, and then he was sent to school. Although he received most of his education in Montreal, he may also have spent some time in Scotland with his father's relatives.

Cuthbert Grant returned to the west from Montreal in 1812 with the annual brigade and was posted to Fort Espérance on the Qu'Appelle River under John Pritchard. Because Grant identified himself passionately with the NWC, he came to see the Red River Settlement as a threat to his way of life.

≡:≡

IN 1811, WHILE engaging in the heated exchange of letters in the pages of the *Inverness Journal*, Simon McGillivray had been made a partner in McTavish, McGillivrays & Co., which controlled over 75 percent of the shares of the NWC. The agreement admitting Simon to the company stated that he was to "watch over its interests wherever they may come under his view, whether in Great Britain or in Canada."[18] Besides marketing NWC furs and purchasing trade goods for the NWC, his duties also included lobbying British officials on behalf of the Canadian fur trade.

In 1814, Simon visited Montreal when McTavish, McGillivrays & Co. was being reorganized. By this time, he was the second-largest shareholder in the company, next to his brother William. The company agreement, which had lapsed almost a year earlier, had not been renewed because of the war and now urgently needed updating. During the previous winter, William had run the company with only the assistance of Archibald Norman McLeod and company accountant John McTavish. In the spring, William had provisionally brought in two new partners:

Roderick McKenzie's younger brother Henry, and Thomas Thain, who was related to Edward Ellice. Henry McKenzie had been in charge of Sir Alexander Mackenzie & Co. since his cousin retired to England and had worked for Simon McTavish previously.

When Simon McGillivray arrived in Montreal from London, the members of the McGillivray family living in Canada enjoyed a reunion before getting down to business. In addition to William, three sisters now lived in Canada. Margery was married to NWC partner Angus Shaw; Mary, who was unmarried, had been looking after William's household since his wife's death; and Elizabeth was married to Judge James Reid. (The Angus Shaw named as one of the Métis captains was the son of the Angus Shaw who was married to Margery McGillivray.)

William and Simon had serious differences of opinion regarding the operations of McTavish, McGillivrays & Co.; however, Simon had to bow to his older brother's views. Although Simon was sharply critical of John McTavish's management of the NWC counting house, John, being a McTavish, could not easily be dismissed. It is important to note here that John McTavish and John George McTavish were two different people. John, the accountant, was a nephew of Simon McTavish, while John George McTavish was a son of the chief of Clan McTavish and became a chief factor in the HBC after 1821.

Simon also disapproved of Henry McKenzie. Much later, Simon wrote that in all his dealings with Henry, "I committed but one mistake and that was when, in deference to my brother, I consented to making him a partner in our house for I had set him down as a scoundrel ever since . . . [I first met him] in 1804, but he had so wound himself round my brother before my arrival at Montreal . . . that I could scarcely help myself."[19]

Although the brothers both agreed that Angus Shaw lacked executive ability, they included him as a partner in the newly organized company because he was a family member and their sister was anxious for his promotion and the resulting move to Montreal. On November 1, 1814, the documents were signed, and Simon left for London a few days later.

The labour contract between voyageurs and the firm of McTavish, McGillivrays & Co., likely used from 1804 to 1821, describes what was expected of engagés:

[Engagés are required] to faithfully carry out all that the said bourgeois, or all others representing their persons . . . may lawfully and honestly command, to make their profit, avoid damage, to warn them if he has knowledge [of danger]; and generally [do] all that a good and loyal servant must and is obliged to do, without doing any particular [private] trading; not to leave or quit the said service, under the pain carried by the laws of this province, and the loss of his wages.[20]

The contract also listed specific summer and winter duties, the length of time engagés were to serve and the salary they would receive. The equipment and provisions to be furnished by the NWC were rarely listed in detail, thus providing one area where negotiations could take place between bourgeois and engagé.

Engagés in the North West were frequently moved from one post to another for various reasons, often to do with misconduct. In August 1800, McGillivray sent a voyageur named La Tour from Lake Vermillion to winter at Grand Portage because the people around Lake Vermillion "complained much of his conduct last winter [and their leader] came here on purpose to desire he should not winter on his lands."[21]

The disagreements within the NWC over the actions taken against the settlers by men like Cameron and Greenfield foreshadowed much more serious dissention between the wintering partners and the Montreal agents. Like the engagés, the wintering partners were not always happy with the terms of their contracts.

12 CRISIS AT THE RED RIVER, 1815—16

We took three foreigners prisoners when
We came to the place called Frog, Frog Plain.
They were men who'd come from Orkney,
Who'd come, you see,
To rob our country.

Now we like honourable men did act,
Sent an ambassador—yes, in fact!
"Monsieur Governor! Would you like to stay?
A moment spare—
There's something we'd like to say."

When we went galloping, galloping by
Governor thought that he would try
For to chase and frighten us Bois-Brûlé.
Catastrophe!
Dead on the ground he lay.

⇒ PIERRE FALCON ⇐
FROM "THE BATTLE OF SEVEN OAKS,"
TRANSLATED BY JAMES REANEY

Even though the conflict between the NWC and Lord Selkirk remained unresolved in the spring of 1815, the Colonial Office was reluctant to take any definite action, not wanting to "prejudge the whole question at issue." Lord Bathurst, Secretary of State for the Colonies, wrote to Governor General Sir Gordon Drummond in Quebec, ordering him to inquire about the menace at the Red River and to protect the settlement as far "as can be afforded without detriment to His Majesty's service." Because Drummond was far from the settlement and had no real authority there, he decided to consult with McGillivray. His aide-de-camp wrote McGillivray that "some of the servants of the North West Company are suspected of being concerned in the diabolical plot against Red River" and asking if "there exists in your opinion any reasonable grounds" for concern about the safety of the settlement from "Indian atrocities." He added that if anything untoward did happen, the NWC would be "considered responsible in the eyes of the world."[1]

McGillivray responded to Drummond on June 24, denying "in the most solemn manner, the allegations where upon this shameful accusation is founded." The Nor'Westers had actually saved the settlers from starvation during their first year at the Red River. Had the NWC not given them food, there would have been no need for hostile Natives to destroy the settlement because "hunger alone would have speedily accomplished the work."[2] McGillivray concluded his letter:

> It is a matter of astonishment that the idea of colonization in the Indian country . . . should be tolerated by His Majesty's government . . . If it fails, as it must and ought, numerous innocent individuals will fall a sacrifice to his Lordships' visionary pursuits; and if it succeeds, it must infallibly destroy the Indian trade . . . we cannot remain passive spectators to the violence used to plunder or destroy our property under any . . . authority as was assumed by Mr. MacDonnell . . . If this was to continue, the NWC would assuredly be justified in repelling force by force, and . . . I cannot but consider the rights and property of that body [the NWC] as equally entitled to protection of His Majesty's Government as the Earl of Selkirk's.[3]

Drummond, after he received the above letter, told the HBC representative in Montreal that danger to the lives and property of the settlers arose principally from the conduct of Governor MacDonnell, who had assumed powers that could not possibly "have been vested in him."[4]

Colin Robertson, who had led the settlers back to the Red River and helped rebuild the settlement after Cameron burned it, accused McGillivray and Drummond of having a close relationship that, given Drummond's position, was improper. Robertson told Selkirk that the two men discussed Miles MacDonnell and the settlement familiarly over their wine. This may or may not have been true, but Robertson was extremely hostile to the Nor'Westers and hardly an objective observer.[5]

Simon McGillivray attended the 1815 annual meeting at Fort William in place of William, who was again suffering from ill health. This was Simon's second trip to North America within a year, which suggests that the McGillivrays were seriously concerned about the NWC situation at the time. Three major issues faced the company at this important meeting: competition from John Jacob Astor and the American Fur Company on the Pacific coast, the HBC's continued refusal to give the NWC transportation access to Hudson Bay, and the threat from Selkirk and the Red River Settlement.

Simon kept a personal account of the 1815 rendezvous. On July 13, everyone was anxious about the late arrival of the Athabasca canoes. Archibald Norman McLeod told Simon that John McGillivray, who was in charge of the Athabasca department, was considered unfit to contend with the expected opposition there. McLeod said that the wintering partners were saying among themselves that John, a first cousin of William and Simon, would not have been left so long as the head of affairs in Athabasca were not his name McGillivray; however, none of them ever had the nerve to openly propose that he be replaced.

On July 15, the Athabasca canoes finally arrived. Duncan Cameron, who was carrying Governor McDonnell and Sheriff John Spencer from the Red River as prisoners to Montreal, also arrived at Fort William that day. Simon McGillivray was part of a group who had gone out to meet the latecomers and accompanied them the final few miles to Fort William.

On July 17, an acrimonious discussion took place between the wintering partners and the agents about the exchange rate, which was the difference in value between British and Halifax currency. The partners thought the agents should absorb the whole loss. As McGillivray put it, "That is to make us pay 20 or 25% for the honour of shipping their returns to England." All the partners disavowed any hostile feelings toward the NWC, but McGillivray told them that "certainly their proposed measures (if not their motives) were of a most hostile character . . . [and] would certainly give great encouragement to the opposition." They might even, Simon said, "go so far as to ruin the NWC." The wintering partners finally backed down.[6]

On July 18 and 19, McGillivray clashed with Dr. John McLoughlin. McLoughlin, who had joined the NWC as physician and apprentice clerk in 1803, had always had an uneasy relationship with the NWC leadership. Now McLoughlin refused to go to Athabasca and said he would retire to Montreal if he was forced to do so. This was despite a unanimous vote posting him to Athabasca. That vote finally was rescinded "on the score of expediency." When it was suggested that McLoughlin go to Lac des Isles instead, McGillivray observed that "it seems he won't go any where unless he can choose for himself." As a result, other partners threatened to quit or to retire in order to have their postings changed. McGillivray concluded that some partners believed "that the country is going to the Devil, and people are acting accordingly. It really appears to me that there are some secret but active enemies of the concern at work in order to sow dissention and if possible destroy the concern." Eventually, McLoughlin backed down on his demands and McGillivray agreed to "omit the minutes about his conduct" in the official record.[7]

The question of John McGillivray came up again, however. The winterers were so dissatisfied with him that, in Simon's words, "Ten partners talk of leaving the country next year and most of them in disgust. There will be the D—to pay if my brother or I do not come up—he should come if possible."[8]

Even though McLoughlin had agreed to go to Athabasca, within a few days he began to neglect his medical duties, causing more dissension. The winterers "as usual" blamed the agents, Simon wrote. As a result, the agents told the winterers to settle the matter as they pleased, and they decided to keep McLoughlin at Fort William.[9]

During the fall of 1815, William McGillivray was so ill from an unnamed condition that he was erroneously reported dead, and Edward Ellice offered to buy a controlling interest in the NWC. Selkirk arrived in

Montreal that fall with authority to negotiate a union between the NWC and the HBC. Due to McGillivray's illness, John Richardson met with Selkirk. The Nor'Westers agreed in advance that they would only discuss union if the NWC were guaranteed charge of "the chief management and direction of the trade in the interior."[10] When Selkirk insisted that the NWC acknowledge the validity of the HBC charter, the negotiations abruptly ended in failure.

During the spring of 1816, Selkirk became much more aggressive. He believed he was lord of Assiniboia as truly as he was proprietor of his Scottish estates, where men were arrested as poachers when they hunted on his land. He wrote to his agent:

The North-West Company must be compelled to quit my lands, especially my post at The Forks. As it will be necessary to use force, I am anxious this should be done under legal warrant. You must give them solemn warning that the land belongs to the Hudson's Bay Company. After this warning, they should not be allowed to cut any timber either for building or fuel. What they have cut should be openly and forcibly seized and their buildings destroyed. They should be treated as poachers. We are so fully advised of the unimpeachable validity of these rights of property, there can be no scruple in enforcing them when you have the physical means.[11]

Robert Semple, who had replaced MacDonnell as governor of the Red River Settlement in the fall of 1815, seized Fort Gibraltar from the Nor'Westers in spring 1816. The following month, Semple issued orders that all NWC employees must leave the Red River, and on June 10 he ordered that Fort Gibraltar be dismantled. The best timber was rafted across the river to be used in rebuilding Fort Douglas and everything else was burned.

Meanwhile, in Montreal, Lady Selkirk had created a powerful social circle in opposition to the NWC elite. Among other comments, Lady Selkirk made cutting remarks about McGillivray's sister Mary and her claims to be "the first lady in Montreal."[12] Because the NWC agents were used to being important members of the Montreal social elite, this was disconcerting to McGillivray, who wrote to a political colleague, likely in late 1815 or early 1816:

What an unfortunate trade we have got into, hemmed in . . . by
a set of unprincipled agents of government on one side and by a
speculating nobleman on the other . . . [Both] as it appears bent
on the same object—to exclude Canada and Canadian subjects
from this too famous trade . . . I really wish I was decently out of
it, although I shall never submit to be kicked out of it by any lord
or commoner in the King's dominions.[13]

In June 1816, McGillivray arrived at Sault Ste. Marie, which had been rebuilt since its destruction during the War of 1812. Awaiting him there were letters from the Red River informing him of the serious events over the winter. He was shocked to learn that Duncan Cameron had been arrested by the HBC and sent to England, that Fort Gibraltar had been destroyed, and that private NWC papers had been seized from an express canoe. McGillivray wrote urgently to his Montreal partners:

God knows what may have taken place in the spring. I almost
tremble to learn the truth . . . Unless government takes a hand
open hostility is inevitable, not only in the Red River but in
other departments, in which case the natives will doubtless get
involved in the quarrel.[14]

As a result of these troubling events, McGillivray requested that Richardson go personally to Quebec to ask that the governor send officers with sufficient authority to keep the peace. Drummond had been replaced as governor by Sir John Sherbrooke in May.

Cuthbert Grant, like Selkirk, was becoming more aggressive. He reported to his fellow Nor'Westers from Fort Qu'Appelle on plans to face the HBC and the settlers: "I am happy to inform you that they [the Métis] are all united and staunch and ready to obey our commands."[15] Led by Grant, the Nor'Westers left Portage la Prairie in mid-June with a load of pemmican that they planned to take to Bas de la Rivière, the NWC post located where the Winnipeg River flows into Lake Winnipeg. There they would transfer the pemmican to the fur brigade from the east for distribution to posts farther north and west of Lake Winnipeg. According to Greenfield's later account, he had ordered Grant to travel by canoe only as far as The Passage, a crossing on the Assiniboine River just within the western edge of modern Winnipeg. At The Passage, Grant was to transfer the pemmican to Red River carts and the men were to travel north cross-country on horseback to avoid being seen by HBC employees and settlers who were close to the river.

Early on the afternoon of June 19, a lookout in the watchtower at Fort Douglas gave the alarm when he caught sight of the party of horsemen riding across the plains. Governor Semple and his men marched out to meet them. The two groups met at Seven Oaks, otherwise known as Frog Plain, soon after. It is not certain which side fired the first shot, but within about fifteen minutes the battle was over, resulting in the deaths of Semple and twenty of his men.[16]

McGillivray had arrived at Fort William just before the Battle of Seven Oaks. Ironically, before learning of the tragedy he wrote to the bourgeois at Lac la Pluie:

> *I consider the injuries last winter sustained have been amply repaid and that we should not do anything without some fresh aggression... The Hudson's Bay people will probably behave with more moderation now ... At all events, let us not be aggressors. We act on the defensive and must defend our property with our best means.*[17]

Now all McGillivray could do was await further news from the Red River and for the arrival of Selkirk from Montreal.

13 THE AFTERMATH OF SEVEN OAKS, 1816–17

The Bois-Brûlé were the new nation,
the Red River was their home
They lived for the buffalo hunt and the pemmican dried and stored
The Métis sons and daughters of the North West Company
Defending their homes and way of life would become their destiny.

. . .

They rode right past Fort Douglas, home of the HBC;
But the battle they won at Seven Oaks was a shallow victory;
De Meurons soldiers soon would seize the heart of the company;
Lord Selkirk and his hired guns fighting in the Pemmican Wars.

⟹ RODNEY BROWN, FROM "PEMMICAN WAR"[1] ⟸

I f anything, the aftermath of the Battle of Seven Oaks was even more controversial than the battle itself. Several different versions of the events that took place at Fort William after Selkirk's arrival there were circulated.

Although it was common knowledge that Selkirk was on his way to the Red River, his arrival at Fort William caught the Nor'Westers by surprise because Selkirk had not taken the route they had expected. According to John Bourke, one of the HBC prisoners taken to Fort William after

Seven Oaks, the Nor'Westers had discussed a plot to either kill or seize Selkirk when he arrived. Bourke claimed to have overheard a conversation between several NWC partners, including Greenfield. The latter assured the other men that the NWC had nothing to fear from Selkirk and, if necessary, he could even be assassinated. Greenfield supposedly named a Métis man who would be willing to shoot Selkirk "while he is asleep, early in the morning."[2] It is not likely that such a plan was ever seriously considered, but it would not be surprising if such a means of ridding the NWC of the bothersome Selkirk had been discussed in jest.

Although McGillivray could not stop Selkirk from travelling to Fort William, he tried to hamper his trip by running him short of provisions. McGillivray engaged a retired Nor'Wester named Daniel McKenzie to buy up all available provisions at Michilimackinac and Drummond Island before Selkirk arrived.

Selkirk left Sault Ste. Marie on August 2 with a party of about one hundred mercenaries plus six regular soldiers of the British 37th Foot led by a man named Sergeant John McNabb. The six soldiers were the only concession that the Colonial Office had been willing to make to Selkirk's request for security, so he hired a private army of demobilized Swiss soldiers known as the Regiment de Meuron, who had served in the British regular army between 1795 and 1816.[3]

On August 12, Selkirk camped near Fort William. He asked Regiment de Meuron commander Captain Proteus D'Orsonnens to deliver a letter to McGillivray. In the letter, Selkirk told McGillivray that, acting in his role as a magistrate, he was inquiring about some men whom he charged had been imprisoned by the Nor'Westers. He demanded that they be released immediately. McGillivray permitted all but two of the men to go to Selkirk's camp, though he denied that they had been held as prisoners. One of the men released was John Pritchard, who appeared at Selkirk's tent to swear an affidavit that he had been imprisoned.

After questioning the men, Selkirk was convinced that he had sufficient evidence to justify legal action against some of the NWC partners, and he made out a warrant to arrest McGillivray. The following day, Selkirk sent two constables and an armed guard of nine men to the fort. The guards were posted by the gate while the constables entered the fort and went to McGillivray's office. McGillivray was there writing a letter and accepted the warrant "as a gentleman," in the words of one of the men who served it. After reading the warrant, he agreed to go with the constables and asked that two other partners be allowed to accompany him to furnish bail. When Selkirk realized that he had three partners in his power instead of one, he refused bail to McGillivray and framed indictments against the other two men. After questioning McGillivray, Selkirk decided that he would be justified in apprehending all of the partners in the fort, so he drew up the necessary papers and sent the constables to arrest the remaining partners.[4]

Selkirk allowed the partners to return to Fort William for the night but insisted that his clerks be allowed to seal up both private and company papers belonging to the NWC. McGillivray agreed, but the job took so long that the clerks were unable to complete it that night. It was after 11 PM before Selkirk's men left. Immediately after, some of the Nor'Westers destroyed many of their papers, including some that had been sealed, and hid arms and ammunition. It does not appear that either action was taken with McGillivray's consent or under his orders.

Despite Selkirk's claims that he had feared a Nor'Westers' attack, McGillivray denied that the NWC had ever seriously considered such an action:

Had the least thought been entertained of making a resistance, nothing would have been easier than to have done so and to have exterminated the whole of Lord Selkirk's band, for . . . we mustered nearly three times the number of his people, and were provided with more than sufficient means of defence, but no such thing was ever attempted, or even suggested.[5]

When Selkirk arrived back in Fort William the next morning, McGillivray handed a formal statement to him and demanded that it be read immediately:

We, the undersigned agents and partners of the North West Company . . . do hereby formally protest against the violent proceedings . . . committed upon our persons and property . . . by a troop of 50 or 60 disbanded and intoxicated soldiers . . . at present in the service and pay of the Earl of Selkirk . . . who forcibly entered the fort gate . . . having their bayonets fixed and shouting . . . which spread general terror amongst the inhabitants . . . [and also sealing] up

the papers and desks in the NWC office and those of the private
rooms of the agents. We do therefore most solemnly protest
against these acts of violence.

[Signed, by McGillivray and seven others.][6]

McGillivray told Selkirk that he did not accept that Semple's killing was murder and that he objected to using the word "massacre" to describe what had happened at Seven Oaks. It was unfortunate that Semple had been killed, but it was a battle, and the Métis had been justified in arming themselves.

Captain D'Orsonnens and Lieutenant Fauché, along with twenty-five soldiers, escorted the constables back to the fort with a search warrant. The Nor'Westers tried to bar the fort gates but the de Meurons sounded a bugle at the first sign of resistance and reinforcements quickly arrived. Upon entering the fort, Selkirk's men discovered that the partners had emptied their files and burned a number of documents in the council room fireplace overnight. They also found four cases of guns and forty fowling pieces, loaded and primed, concealed in a hayloft. When Selkirk learned this, he occupied the fort and removed all the Nor'Westers.

Crucially, in Selkirk's view, among the papers found was a list containing the names of all the men at Seven Oaks. All but thirteen of the names had been marked off "as having received habillements [clothing]." Twenty bales of habillements were also found, along with an invoice containing the thirteen names that had not been marked off the list. These discoveries convinced Selkirk that he had a case for conspiracy. Undoubtedly, it was with great satisfaction that he wrote to Upper Canada's Attorney General D'Arcy Boulton on August 17 that he was sending him "a cargo of criminals of a larger calibre than usually came before the courts at York."[7]

Gaspard Adolph Fauché, a former Regiment de Meuron lieutenant, wrote an account of his participation in the events at Fort William.[8] According to Fauché, after interviewing McGillivray and deciding to arrest the other partners who were still in the fort, Selkirk sent over the constable with warrants, accompanied by about twenty-five men in two boats. Between two and three hundred Natives and Canadians were standing outside the fort's main gate, and the partners stood in the gateway. The constable proceeded to issue the warrants, but John McDonald of

Garth declared that he would not submit to the warrant or allow anyone to enter the fort until McGillivray was liberated. When the Nor'Westers tried to force the gate shut, the men in the boats rushed forward and cleared their way through to the gate. The constable ordered the men to arrest McDonald, "who was exceedingly violent," and put him in one of the boats. At that, the other partners peacefully submitted.

The partners were taken before Selkirk, who questioned them and then allowed them to return to their rooms in the fort for the night "upon the condition that they would not attempt any hostilities, to which they pledged their word of honour." Selkirk then ordered that all NWC documents be sealed.

The next morning, Fauché learned that a canoe had left the fort during the night loaded with ammunition and arms and that many papers had been burned by the partners. Selkirk's men found eight barrels of gunpowder that had been taken out of the powder magazine and some "apparently freshly loaded and primed" guns hidden under some hay. This seemed to indicate that the NWC employees were planning to attack; therefore, most of them were sent across the river and their canoes were confiscated.

On August 18, the prisoners, under the control of Fauché, were put into three canoes to be taken to York in Upper Canada. About a week later, they lost nine men and one of the canoes. They had stopped for dinner at an island about fifteen miles from Sault Ste. Marie. The wind came up while they were eating, but because they were on the lee side of the island they didn't realize how strong it was. According to Fauché, he asked McGillivray, "whom I invariably consulted during our voyage," if he felt it was safe to continue on. McGillivray said that there should "not be the least danger if the guides of the canoes did their duty." Once they got the canoes away from the island, they realized how strong the wind was, but it was too late to go back. They proceeded under close-reefed sails and steered for the first point of land. When they neared it, one of the canoes upset in the shoals and nine men were drowned. "It is unnecessary however, to further defend myself, as I have sufficient witnesses to testify that I consulted Mr. McGillivray and followed his advice," Fauché stated.

On September 3, Fauché arrived at York with the prisoners, but they were sent on to Kingston because the Attorney General had gone there on his circuit. After Fauché missed him at Kingston, he followed him to Brockville. There, the prisoners applied for a writ of habeas corpus, so Fauché had to take them to Montreal, where they arrived on September 10. The prisoners were allowed out on bail almost immediately.

Another man agreed with Fauché's description of the events at Fort William, but not with his description of the canoe accident. This account stated that the guides disagreed with McGillivray and did not want to leave the island; however, their views were disregarded. When the lead canoe capsized, the other canoes were so heavily laden that they had to put in to shore to offload some of their cargo before returning to the rescue.[9]

McGillivray himself said nothing about being consulted by Fauché about leaving the island, but he was exceedingly angry about the way Selkirk expected them to travel east. Although construction of several new canoes was almost completed, Selkirk refused to make use of them. Not surprisingly, he also replaced the regular voyageur crews with Iroquois paddlers whom he paid. There is little doubt, however, that the canoes were badly overloaded and may not have been in the best repair.

According to Sergeant John McNabb of the British 37th Regiment of Foot, who wrote of the events at Fort William, "Much praise is due to Captain D'Orsonnens, for his cool and determined conduct. Lieutenant Fauche co-operated with the most laudable zeal and correctness, and the men behaved with the most exemplary propriety."[10]

The account of de Meuron lieutenant von Graffenried is likely closest to the truth: "Because the soldiers were dressed half in uniform and half in civilian clothes, and we the officers wore short jackets and were armed with swords and pistols, we resembled a band of robbers . . . Our men, however, were in no mood to fool around and broke down the gate. Fortunately no shot was fired, otherwise we could not have prevented our men from plundering, and in all likelihood blood would have been spilled."[11]

Angus Shaw wrote a detailed report giving the NWC version of events at both Seven Oaks and Fort William. Shaw said that when Governor Semple saw a party led by Cuthbert Grant pass by the HBC fort, he ordered his men to arm themselves and go out to attack them. Semple went out with about twenty-six officers and men and one cannon. When the two groups approached each other, a parley took place, "but it is incontestably proven that Mr. Semple ordered his men to fire in the first instance, by which fire one Indian was killed and a half-breed mortally wounded. This fire was unfortunately so successfully returned that in a few minutes Mr. Semple, 4 officers, and 19 men were left dead on the spot."[12] Shaw stated that, after the battle, the Natives told the colonists to leave the country immediately and never again to return. They were resolved never to permit any whites to settle on their land, which they had not sold to the king or Lord Selkirk.

According to Shaw's report, accounts of the catastrophe reached Selkirk on his way to the Red River. At the time, he was accompanied by about 150 well-armed soldiers who also had ten or twelve cannons. On his arrival at Fort William, Selkirk sent "a warrant from himself as a magistrate for the Indian Territory, who apprehended Mr. McGillivray . . . with all such partners as might be useful in carrying on the business." Selkirk with his foreign soldiers then took possession of the depot of Fort William and in a couple of days sent down the NWC gentlemen as prisoners. By means of his forces, Selkirk retained possession of the depot and would not permit the furs, to the amount of fifty thousand pounds sterling, to be removed. Likewise, Selkirk got possession of goods and provisions to the amount of sixty thousand pounds and turned "those of our servants and clerks out of doors who would not enter his service, in short acting as if the whole place and property were his own, tho' it is situated 800 miles from the nearest limits of the Hudson's Bay territory."[13]

Shaw concluded by saying that McGillivray and company were placed on bail until March 1817, when they were to be tried for "aiding and abetting the Indians and half-breeds" who in their own defence killed several people at Seven Oaks. These charges, Shaw said, were made "despite the fact that the event took place more than a thousand miles from where those gentlemen were at the time this unfortunate event took place."[14]

Before being taken from Fort William under arrest, McGillivray sent an express canoe off in an attempt to procure a warrant for Selkirk's arrest. The unnamed man sent by McGillivray was able to get a warrant from the Justice of the Peace at Drummond's Island, who dispatched a constable to serve the warrant on Selkirk. When the constable arrived, Selkirk resisted arrest and later told authorities that he had done so because he believed the warrant was "a trick" and the constable "an impostor."[15]

As soon as McGillivray arrived in Montreal and was released on bail, he tried to send a brigade to Fort William, but the fall gales on Lake Superior forced it to turn back. About this time, Selkirk apparently admitted in a letter to Governor Sherbrooke that he had attacked Fort William with the intention of ruining the NWC by tying up its capital until the differences between the NWC and the HBC were settled. Because McGillivray had not been allowed to take his furs to Montreal for sale that summer, he was forced to appeal to John Jacob Astor for a loan.

McGillivray also learned that the de Meurons had attacked two South West Company posts and arrested James Grant, agent at Fond du Lac. They seized several thousand pounds sterling in goods from Fond du Lac and sent them to Fort William. Although Grant was sent to York under arrest, he was quickly released when the warrant was found to be illegal because he was in the United States at the time of his arrest.

In the spring of 1817, Simon McGillivray arrived from London. As soon as the ice went out, Simon and William set off for Fort William with a brigade of six canoes. When they arrived there on May 29, Selkirk had already left for the Red River. He had left instructions that no one but the commissioners appointed by the government to investigate the NWC–HBC dispute should be allowed access to the fort, but McGillivray demanded the fort's keys. He then confined the two men left in charge by Selkirk, Sheriff John Spencer and Sergeant John McNabb, in separate rooms under guard. The guard accompanied the men, even "to the necessary." Soon after, a sign offering a reward of fifty pounds for the capture of Lord Selkirk appeared on the main gate of Fort William.

The NWC was in a desperate state by the time McGillivray arrived at Fort William. Selkirk had seized about £100,000 worth of furs, and Astor was asserting rights south of the forty-ninth parallel. Over the winter, Selkirk had treated everything in Fort William, including McGillivray's private quarters, as if they were his own. That was undoubtedly galling to McGillivray, but he quickly learned of much more serious actions taken by Selkirk. People at nearby posts had been denied supplies already baled and labelled for them, causing considerable hardship. The de Meuron mercenaries had captured Lac la Pluie and then recaptured Fort Douglas.

They had also plundered the provisions at Bas de la Rivière on Lake Winnipeg, completely disrupting the NWC supply chain. This would create serious, as yet unimagined, problems.

On May 1, a royal proclamation was issued that required all parties in the dispute to refrain from further hostilities and to restore all posts and goods seized during the past conflicts, but some months would pass before everyone would learn about the proclamation, let alone take action to obey it.

Selkirk was not the only official visitor to the Red River in the summer of 1817. William Coltman also visited in his capacity as head of an official government commission to inquire into the events surrounding Seven Oaks. In February 1818, written proposals were exchanged between McGillivray and Selkirk through Coltman. McGillivray proposed that the HBC withdraw from Athabasca country and the NWC would pay for any goods the HBC left there. In return, the NWC would withdraw from the Red River, although it would continue to hold the upper Assiniboine. Claims for civil damages were to be submitted to four "intelligent merchants," two for each side, with an umpire in case of disagreement. All criminal charges were to be waived. Selkirk, in return, denied that he had any connection with Athabasca and strongly opposed waiving criminal charges.[16]

Selkirk's actions at Fort William were passed over as discreetly as possible by his supporters and condemned unsparingly by his opponents. His feelings were vehemently expressed in a letter in which he wrote that the NWC, "with the exception of the slave traders, are perhaps the most unprincipled men who ever had to boast of support and countenance from the British Government." Because he could find no one else willing to make the arrests, Selkirk had decided to do it himself in the capacity of magistrate. "In the delicate position in which I stand as a party interested," he wrote to Governor Sherbrooke from the Sault on July 29, 1816, "I could have wished that some other magistrate should have undertaken the investigation."[17]

A dispatch, likely written by Parliamentary Under-Secretary Henry Goulburn to Attorney General Uniacke of Lower Canada in February 1817, strongly criticized Selkirk for his "resistance to the execution of the warrants issued against him for false imprisonment":

Lord Selkirk has rendered himself doubly amenable to the laws;
and it is necessary . . . that the determination of the Government
to enforce the law with respect to all . . . should be effectually
and speedily evinced. You will therefore, without delay on
the receipt of this instruction, take care that an indictment be
preferred against his Lordship, . . . and, upon a true bill being
found against him, you will take the necessary measures in such
cases for arresting his Lordship, and bringing him before the
court from which the process issued.[18]

John Strachan, an Anglican clergyman and a close friend of a number of Nor'Westers, including William McGillivray, also strongly attacked Selkirk in a pamphlet entitled "A letter to the Rt. Hon. The Earl of Selkirk on His Settlement at the Red River Near Hudson's Bay." It must be kept in mind, however, that Strachan got most of the information on which he based his attack directly from McGillivray. Strachan described Selkirk as a "damnable land speculator, who in order to charge exorbitant prices for real estate at Red River, had enticed unsuspecting immigrants into the dreary wilderness." He also demanded that Selkirk "suffer the punishment of the law" for having pillaged innocent immigrants.[19] Later, Selkirk came to bitterly regret his actions at Fort William because they had led to so much criticism.

In 1818, eighteen true bills of indictment were found against the NWC. The charges ranged from murder to conspiracy. There were 35 charges against NWC partners, including William and Simon McGillivray, and 135 charges against other NWC employees. In September, four other bills were added and all the cases were moved to Upper Canada, along with the cases against Selkirk.[20]

McGillivray sent the following statement to Coltman:

[At the beginning of the recent disturbances] we did not see in
the measures of Lord Selkirk any other than the effects of an
enthusiastic prosecution of his Lordship's visionary schemes,
which . . . might perhaps [have] been ascribed to laudable
motives; nor did we see, in the increasing activity of the
HBC traders anything more than an unwonted ebullition of
commercial rivalry, which, however much it was in our interests

to counteract, we never could entertain thoughts of repressing by other means than by a commensurate increase of energy and of industry in the operations of our trade.[21]

McGillivray went on to say, however, that he soon concluded that Selkirk was determined to destroy the NWC "and ultimately raise himself upon the ruins of the NWC into a monopolizer of the fur trade of the whole continent, in addition to his ambition of becoming lord paramount of the soil, through an immense tract of country." He then complained about the delays in going to trial. Attorney General Uniacke was not sympathetic. He wrote that McGillivray might have saved His Excellency "this needless repetition of the statement" and that the NWC partners "must be sensible that justice has been done them." He also hoped that "in future they will not avail themselves of the ingenuity of their legal advisers to incriminate His Majesty's government and its officers."[22]

McGillivray responded angrily:

To this I shall only reply that the partners of the NWC are sensible that justice has not been done them and that Mr. Attorney-General need not cherish the hope that either the great power of his office, or of his attempt to identify himself with His Majesty's Government, will deter them from complaining of injustices by whomsoever inflicted, or repelling misrepresentations by whomever advanced.[23]

McGillivray was again in poor health in the spring of 1818. He remained ill over the entire summer, possibly with rheumatic fever. So many winterers and clerks were still under bail or in custody that it was going to be difficult to man even the most important posts in the coming year. The case between the NWC and Selkirk was finally to proceed at Sandwich in early September, but because William was not well enough to attend, Simon went in his place. This was a worry to William, who feared Simon's hot temper would get him into trouble during the trial. The case dragged on. Selkirk was present, but ill with the tuberculosis that would kill him a few years later. Matters worsened when William's concerns about Simon's temper proved well founded, and Simon was accused of assaulting a police officer. The members of the jury were unable to reach a verdict, so the judge dismissed them.

Neither the NWC nor Selkirk was happy with this outcome, but they went on to prepare for the fall assizes at York, where Robert Semple's death would be examined. By this time, William was well enough to attend court, but Selkirk left for England. At York, the two NWC engagés charged with Semple's death were acquitted. As well, charges against both William and almost all of the winterers were dropped.

14 THE NORTH WEST COMPANY AND THE PACIFIC TRADE, 1795—1815

The mountains call me now, the rivers talk to me

. . .

Like Mackenzie and Fraser an explorer I'll be
I'll trace the shores, I'll draw the lines,
I'll be the eyes of the company
For no longer will I take my charge with the
English Lords of the HBC
On the trail of the Canadians, it's a Nor'Wester I'll be.

⇒ RODNEY BROWN ⇐
FROM "MAP OF DREAMS," A SONG ABOUT DAVID THOMPSON[1]

During the conflict between Selkirk and the NWC that dominated the period from 1810 to 1818, the NWC also was engaged in trade on the Pacific coast and with China. This trade had its beginnings in the 1790s and was inextricably connected with the Americans and John Jacob Astor in particular. Although much of the border between American and British territories was decided with the signing of the Jay Treaty in 1794, the boundary at the Pacific coast was not finally settled until 1846.

Alexander Henry the Elder had become interested in the China fur trade as early as the 1780s. He passed on his ideas, which he called "my favourite plan," to his friend John Jacob Astor and introduced him into the Canadian fur trade.[2] Astor sometimes carried furs from the NWC to the China market and bought British trade goods, which Native trappers preferred to goods manufactured in the United States. The NWC found it advantageous to work with Astor on the American side of the Great Lakes to avoid American regulations regarding foreigners trading there; as a result, the South West Company was organized. Despite this association, the Nor'Westers continued to suspect that their interests and those of Astor were not completely compatible.

The East India Company created the same kinds of problems for the NWC in trading with China as the HBC did in North American trade. In the mid-1790s, Astor learned that the governor of the East India Company had a connection with Astor's home village in Germany. As a result of exploiting this tenuous connection, Astor obtained permission to trade in any ports under the East India Company monopoly; thus, he and Alexander Henry were able to build up a profitable trade with China.

In November 1795, Henry wrote to Simon McTavish in London to tell him that Astor was planning to go to London that fall. Henry believed that Astor wished to meet with McTavish to make some proposals regarding the disposal of NWC furs in New York. As a result, Henry wrote, he hoped to hear from McTavish on this topic and that he relied "on your friendship in the business."[3]

Some months previously, in May, James Hallowell had written to McTavish from Montreal to say that William McGillivray had just arrived from London with a copy of the China accounts that McTavish had asked him to deliver. Hallowell grumbled that he had not attempted to examine the accounts because "I have found it a laborious business having nobody to apply to for explanations." He said that if McTavish, Fraser & Co. had given the dealings with China an accounting in their books, "it would have cost but little trouble there" and "it would have saved an infinite deal here." He concluded that if he understood the accounts correctly, "there will be a loss of £15,000 sterling on the two first [China] adventures."[4]

In his letter, Hallowell also discussed the possible need to have an American citizen in the New York branch of the NWC because of the naturalization bill passed in the last session of the American Congress. Hallowell apparently thought that Astor should be brought into the NWC:

I wish Astor may arrive from Europe before we are obliged to determine. He may . . . by the connections he may make on the continent be able to throw an equivalent into the house for the share he may draw. It was a favourite idea of mine before we learnt how far you had gone with Mackenzie if that either William or I might be able to supply whatever is defective in the capacity of Mr. Astor for conducting the business with the greatest advantage & respectability, & such I know is the aid he would above all others prefer.[5]

Astor had founded the American Fur Company in 1808 and the Pacific Fur Company two years later. Half of the Pacific Fur Company stock was held by Astor through the American Fur Company, which was owned exclusively by Astor, who provided all of the capital. The other half of the stock was ascribed to working partners or kept in reserve. In 1811, the company built a trading post at Astoria, located in present-day Oregon. Astor's plan included a permanent settlement at the mouth of the Columbia River and a trade ring including New York, Russian Alaska, Hawaii, and China.

Astor offered the NWC a share in the Pacific Fur Company. The wintering partners were considering accepting the offer, but Simon McGillivray was strongly opposed. He said:

If you do not oppose the Americans beyond the mountains they will bye and bye meet you on this side; and even if you should ultimately be inclined to make an amicable arrangement with them, the only way to do so upon an independent footing, or to obtain good terms, is to have rival establishments previously formed in the country on the same footing as theirs.[6]

As a result of Simon's views, the NWC refused Astor's offer of a half-interest in the Pacific Fur Company, "having no desire to extend the territories of the US," and they decided at their 1811 rendezvous that

David Thompson "should be left to prosecute his plans of discovery on the west side of the Rocky Mountains towards the Pacific."[7]

The NWC had been formally lobbying the British government since 1810 for a twenty-one-year monopoly on trade in all parts of the British North West not claimed by the HBC. A petition with that request was read before the Prince Regent at Whitehall on June 22, 1811, and passed on to the Board of Trade for consideration. After passing the request on from one department to another, the government finally denied the NWC a charter on the grounds that it might infringe on American territorial rights; however, it did not explain what it meant by that statement.

The NWC also asked for permission from the East India Company to export furs directly to Canton. In November 1810, Simon McGillivray had written to the secretary of state for war and colonies (Lord Liverpool) calling for a British warship to be sent to the Columbia to prevent an American takeover of the region. He said that "the ultimate right of possession of the whole northwest coast of America"[8] was at stake. At the 1811 rendezvous, the NWC voted to send a brigade of sixty men to the Columbia to compete with the Americans.

In 1811, a pamphlet titled *On the Origin and Progress of the North-West Company of Canada* was published with the aim of furthering the efforts of the NWC to obtain a charter for exclusive trade on the Pacific coast. The authorship of the pamphlet was credited to Nathaniel Atcheson, although it may have been written by Duncan McGillivray or a man named John Henry. At the very least, it seems likely that Duncan provided Atcheson with information. The pamphlet's author argued that the interests of the NWC and the improvement of the condition of the Natives "are reciprocally dependent upon each other." In order for the NWC to obtain the greatest possible quantity of furs from the trade, it must "necessarily endeavour to maintain peace and sobriety among the Indians, and to induce them to devote their attention entirely to the chase." If the Natives, because of either real or imaginary ill usage, determined to seize unsold trade goods or injure traders, the traders would have no protection. Furthermore, a solitary trader might acquire an instant benefit by "an act of villainy" if he left the country immediately afterward, but "the interests of the Company require a continuance of trade from year to year."[9]

The NWC was also, the pamphlet's author argued, the only connection most remote Natives had with the British government, and they regarded traders as "representatives of His Majesty." He stated, "Unless prevented by the timely interference of the British government, the Trade will be lost, to not the North West Company only, but to Great Britain; and with the trade, the British influence over the Indians." Clearly, the NWC feared losing all to the Americans.[10]

—≥:≡—

BY THE SPRING of 1812, William McGillivray was exceedingly frustrated in his dealings with both the East India Company and the British government. The East India Company did not want to lose its eastern trade monopoly, so it was trying to prevent the NWC from obtaining a licence to trade in China, and the government would not give him a straight answer to his petition for a charter for the NWC.

The NWC had been seriously considering the trade with China over the past few years. In 1810, David Thompson had been requested to complete his reconnaissance of the Columbia River so that the NWC could determine the feasibility of establishing a fur trade west of the Rockies. Although Thompson found that the Columbia was navigable, by the time he reached its mouth in 1811, he found the Americans already there and building Fort Astoria. He finally completed his report for the NWC in July 1812.

At the 1811 Fort William rendezvous, the agents and wintering partners had begun making formal plans for the China trade. They realized that it would be very expensive to launch such a project. McGillivray had convinced a senior partner named Donald McTavish, a first cousin to Simon McTavish, to postpone his retirement in order to take command of the Columbia enterprise. McGillivray was responsible for negotiating with the East India Company, ordering provisions and trade goods, and engaging a ship and its captain.

The NWC plan for the China trade involved fitting out a ship for a voyage of two to three years. It would deliver European trade goods at the Columbia River for beaver skins. The furs would be taken to China, where they would be traded for either Chinese goods or for money. Finally, the ship would return to England to sell the goods or invest the money. Then the whole cycle would begin again. Unfortunately for the NWC, the plan failed for a number of reasons.

For over two hundred years, the charter of "The Company of Merchants of London trading into the East Indies"—the original name of the East India Company—had given it exclusive trading rights throughout the Indian and Pacific Oceans. The Indiamen were jealous of their prerogatives, which made it difficult to acquire a licence to trade in Canton. McGillivray erroneously thought that the NWC and the East India Company were close to an agreement, telling the wintering partners in April 1812 that "the East India Company appear to be still favourably disposed—the certainty of getting dollars in Canton for our beaver skins removed a barrier which last year I thought insurmountable."[11]

In January 1813, the NWC finally did receive the long-awaited licence; however, the terms were decidedly unfavourable to the NWC, which was barred from trading beaver skins for Chinese goods and also was not allowed to transport specie (coins). Rather, the Nor'Westers had to settle for bills of exchange, which did not appreciate in value as specie might, and they would have to wait for payment for a whole year after the bills of exchange were presented. Simon McGillivray and Donald McTavish did not seem to realize just how unfavourable the East India Company contract was to the NWC when they signed it. As he was no longer in London at this time, William did not sign.

The East India Company did deign to allow *Isaac Todd* to transport cargo belonging to them for freight money. The three-masted *Isaac Todd* had been built for the NWC at Trois Rivières, Quebec, in 1811 and was owned by John McTavish. It weighed about 350 tons and had a crew of seventeen. *Isaac Todd* left Montreal for England on its maiden voyage on August 18, 1812. After its cargo of furs was unloaded at the London docks, the ship was outfitted for the long voyage back to British Columbia, then on to China and back to London via the Indian and Atlantic Oceans. Despite the fact that the ship had only completed one Atlantic crossing, while in London *Isaac Todd* was completely refurbished and modified to accommodate twenty cannons. Because the War of 1812 was currently being waged, the Nor'Westers successfully petitioned the British government for a letter of marque[12] and a man-of-war to escort *Isaac Todd*. They were not successful, however, in getting the company charter that they had pursued for so long. A frustrated Simon McGillivray wrote to the wintering partners, "It is impossible that you can fully understand or that I can . . . explain to you the trouble and difficulty which attend applications to government or public bodies in this country."[13]

By February 1813, *Isaac Todd* was completely outfitted and ready to leave for Portsmouth, where it would rendezvous with the Atlantic convoy, which included both merchant and naval ships. Donald McTavish and John McDonald of Garth travelled on the ship and were in charge of the expedition. Once they arrived at Portsmouth, they were delayed another month awaiting final government clearance. While waiting, six Canadian voyageurs and several clerks on *Isaac Todd* were captured by a press gang for the Royal Navy. Edward Ellice, who was related by marriage to the port admiral, got the men released.

Government approval for the naval escort did not arrive early enough for *Isaac Todd* to reach the Columbia River in May 1813 as planned. On March 25, *Isaac Todd* finally left Portsmouth with the East India Company fleet as part of a group of about forty merchant ships plus a naval squadron.

The NWC tried to convince the British officials that they needed a convoy across the Pacific as well as the Atlantic. While the Nor'Westers may have been guilty of some hyperbole, they insisted that "the territorial possession of the countries bordering on the Columbia River, and finally the whole Northwest coast of the continent of America, will depend upon the measures to be adopted by His Majesty's government on the present occasion."[14] The secretary for war and the colonies, Lord Bathurst, agreed.

Isaac Todd safely reached the Columbia River and continued on to China, finally arriving at Macao Roads in China late in 1814. Chinese trade with westerners was very expensive and strictly regulated. Although *Isaac Todd* was in China until March 13, 1815, the crew was only allowed two days of shore leave during their stay. In addition to Chinese restrictions, the terms of the East India Company licence made it impossible for the Nor'Westers to profit from their Chinese trade. The NWC furs were purchased on its behalf by the East India Company agent who gave a bill of exchange to the captain for the proceeds plus nominal interest. The captain then presented the bill to the proper authorities in England for payment. The licence also required *Isaac Todd* to transport some three hundred tons of cargo for the East India Company (tea and fabric), for which the NWC received £5,040 or 16 guineas per ton.

As early as June 19, 1815, William McGillivray wrote from Montreal conceding that *Isaac Todd* would lose nearly £15,000 on the China venture. The beaver had sold sluggishly in Canton for $3.80 to $3.90 each, far below what they had hoped for. He could only hope the remaining unsold beaver sold for a better price to offset some of this loss. *Isaac Todd* completed a circumnavigation of the globe and arrived back in London on September 20, 1815. The ship would ultimately be sold for £2,270, somewhat reducing the loss McGillivray had estimated. By the time *Isaac Todd* arrived in London, the NWC had already purchased two other ships (*Columbia* and *Colonel Allan*), but there would be no more. Almost all future shipping was placed in the hands of the American shipping company J. & T.H. Perkins of Boston. McGillivray wrote to one of the wintering partners: "The expense attending the sending of our own vessels to China is too heavy—and the partners of the NWC do not understand the management of ships or captains; soliciting and trading skins is their real business."[15]

Although the voyage of *Isaac Todd* was almost a total failure, the NWC proprietors continued with the China trade for six more years with persistent losses before giving it up. During these years, they paid American vessels one-quarter of the net proceeds to transport their beaver.

15 ATHABASCA COUNTRY AND THE LAST YEARS OF THE NORTH WEST COMPANY, 1818—20

Out of the night and the north;
Savage of breed and of bone,
Shaggy and swift comes the yelping band,
Freighters of fur from the voiceless land
That sleeps in the Arctic zone.

Laden with skins from the north,
Beaver and bear and raccoon,
Marten and mink from the polar belts,
Otter and ermine and sable pelts—
The spoils of the hunter's moon.

E. PAULINE JOHNSON, FROM "THE TRAIN DOGS"

In October 1818, Colin Robertson arrived at Fort Wedderburn in Athabasca country to re-establish the HBC in the fur trade there. Robertson wrote a series of letters to the members of the Committee of the Honourable Hudson's Bay Company giving his take on the Athabasca country struggle. He described the bad relations that existed between the HBC and the Nor'Westers from the day he arrived there.

Samuel Black was an NWC clerk who seemed to serve the same function for the NWC as an enforcer does on a modern hockey team. Robertson wrote, "Black is now in his glory, leading a parcel of bullies, who come over every evening in a body calling out our men to fight pitched battles." The local Natives camped nearby put the NWC "bullies at defiance and boldly came forward to congratulate me on my arrival on their lands." Robertson gave them a glass, made a speech, and in return most of them promised to bring him their furs in the spring.[1]

Shortly after his arrival, Robertson was talking with William McGillivray's son Simon, who was usually referred to as Simon McGillivray Jr. to distinguish him from his uncle. Suddenly, Black and eight or ten other men surrounded Robertson. In the struggle, according to Robertson, his pistol fell from his pocket and went off while he was trying to pick it up. Black and his men, who claimed that Robertson had brandished the pistol at them, dragged Robertson to the beach and forced him into a canoe. He was taken to Fort Chipewyan, where he was confined for the winter, although he was able to correspond with his men by a cipher transmitted inside the bung hole of a small keg filled with rum. While Robertson was being taken back to Canada under guard in the spring of 1819, he managed to escape at Cumberland House and returned to lead the Athabasca expedition later that year.

About the same time as Robertson escaped custody, a group of Nor'Westers was arrested by William Williams, the new governor-in-chief of Rupert's Land, at Grand Rapids on Lake Winnipeg. Williams had mustered a force of thirty men plus heavy weapons and captured the Nor'Westers as they walked across the portage while their canoes shot the rapids. The arrests were made under warrants of dubious legality. The prisoners, including seven NWC partners, were taken to York Factory by Williams and Robertson. Two prisoners escaped; one of them, Joseph Frobisher's son Benjamin, was recaptured and suffered severe head injuries when he was beaten for protesting Governor Williams's actions. His death less than two years later at the age of thirty-nine was blamed on the beating. The remaining prisoners were taken to England for trial but were released for lack of a prosecutor.

≡:≡

DISSENSION HAD BEEN simmering among the NWC wintering partners for years, but it reached a peak at the 1819 Fort William rendezvous. The wintering partners were angry that most of the money used to pay the legal bills from the conflict with Selkirk and the HBC had been found by using funds owed to them. Shortly after the rendezvous, secret preliminary discussions began in an attempt to end the bitter antagonism between the HBC and the NWC.

Selkirk's lawyer, Samuel Gale, wrote to Lady Selkirk on September 20, 1819, saying that McGillivray had been unsuccessful in inducing the wintering partners to prolong or renew their partnership agreement, which was soon to expire. McGillivray left Fort William "in a melancholy mood, but is determined next summer to make further attempts to obtain a renewal of the partnership without which the whole . . . concern would be annihilated."[2]

One of the wintering partners, almost certainly John McLoughlin or his representative, consulted with Gale, asking that his name be kept confidential. He asked Gale if the partners could obtain their outfits from the HBC and be sanctioned to trade by that body "on condition of sending their returns of furs to the HBC" if they refused to renew their contracts with the NWC. He requested Gale to "learn as much in detail as possible the most favourable terms the HBC would be likely to give the wintering partners," and concluded, "I should like to have the answer on this subject as soon as possible in order that my friend may give information to his correspondent by the first conveyance after the opening of the navigation and before any meeting take place at For William."[3] Gale, naturally, could not commit himself to any agreement; however, he thought it very likely that the HBC would have no objection.

Gale told Lady Selkirk that the wintering partners could not be looked upon in the same light as the other partners. "The latter are the great criminals . . . the favoured of Government and for whom the Government has disgraced itself. Anything but perpetual hostility to the Montreal and London agency houses would disgrace the HBC."[4]

The majority of the wintering partners did not become aware of the financial problems of the NWC until the 1820 rendezvous, despite the fact that there had been discontent among the winterers for many years. Convinced that McLoughlin and other dissidents were meeting behind his back, McGillivray transferred McLoughlin from Fort William just before the meeting began and replaced him with John George McTavish.

That pre-emptive move proved unsuccessful, as eighteen of the partners authorized McLoughlin and Angus Bethune to negotiate with the HBC in London on their behalf.

≡:≡

IN JUNE 1820, Colin Robertson left Athabasca country, heading east. Concerned that he might be waylaid by the NWC, he wrapped both his private papers and those belonging to the HBC in waterproof cloth and hid the package in a bag of pemmican. His concern was not misplaced, as he was arrested at Grand Rapids on June 18 and taken to Fort William by NWC partner John Duncan Campbell. According to Robertson, Campbell, "a loquacious gentleman," told him that McGillivray had assured the Nor'Westers that "a union is just upon the eve of being formed," but that the HBC "must be forced to terms" by driving them from Île-à-la-Crosse and Athabasca, and "a number of extra men had been engaged for that purpose."[5]

Robertson arrived at Fort William on July 30 and sent a note to McGillivray requesting to know upon what authority he had been arrested and when he could expect to be taken to court. McGillivray declined to provide that information, as it "would answer no other purpose than furnish an additional document to be produced in court." A few days later, Robertson and McGillivray had a conversation in which Robertson quoted McGillivray as saying "in very strong terms" that "if no reconciliation takes place between the two companies, the country would be ruined for both." When Robertson asked if negotiations had been "entered into at home," McGillivray replied that the NWC had made several overtures that were rejected by the late Lord Selkirk. He went on to say that he hoped that the HBC committee would take a more liberal view of matters and be less exorbitant in their demands.[6]

Robertson later commented on his conversation with McGillivray, saying that the NWC hopes "are fixed on a union alone. Their capturing business is attended with a very heavy expense . . . As to the legality or illegality of their measures, that gives them no concern if the object can only be attained. Were the HBC to act on similar principles, these people could be crushed in one season."[7]

After being kept "under close confinement" at Fort William from July 30 to August 13, Robertson was taken to Lower Canada. From there he

Colin Robertson, who was determined to expand the HBC fur trade into Athabasca country, was arrested by the Nor'Westers in 1818 and again in 1820. LIBRARY AND ARCHIVES CANADA ACCESSION NO. 1958-186-1, C-00894

escaped to the United States and thence to England. Robertson was not directly involved with the amalgamation of the NWC and HBC and actually was opposed to the coalition, even though his determined assaults on the Athabasca between 1816 and 1820 were major factors in breaking down the Nor'Westers' opposition to union.[8]

In the fall of 1820, Robertson travelled to England on the same ship as NWC partners John McLoughlin and Angus Bethune. Also aboard was John Caldwell, receiver-general of Lower Canada and a close friend of William McGillivray. Caldwell told Robertson that McGillivray regretted exceedingly the Grand Rapids business and the arrest of Robertson and added that even though McGillivray was the head of the NWC, his opinions were frequently overruled. At first Robertson assumed that the "drift of this conversation was to prevent my applying to the proper authorities in London for redress." He soon discovered his mistake. When he asked Caldwell about the purpose of McLoughlin and Bethune's visit to London, Caldwell replied, "Come, come, Mr. R., that's too bad. You know very well, as you are going to introduce them to the HBC."

Robertson suddenly realized that McLoughlin and Bethune were working against McGillivray, and this was confirmed soon after when Dr. McLoughlin came to see Robertson. Obviously embarrassed, McLoughlin stumbled rather awkwardly upon an inquiry as to the character of the gentlemen of the HBC committee, "if they were affable and easy in their manners."

The delighted Robertson replied, "You will see them doctor, by and bye, and you will tell us all about it yourself."

"Me, me," stammered the poor doctor, with a face as red as a full moon in a frosty morning, "How, how am I going to see them?"[9] Within a few months, McLoughlin would discover the answer to this question.

≡:≡

ONE OF THE other traders arrested during the HBC–NWC conflict was Simon McGillivray Jr. During his imprisonment in 1820–21 at Fort Chipewyan in Athabasca country, he kept a diary, which was found in England in 1957. It is likely that Simon, who was in London at the time of his father's death, gave it to his father. The following details come from this diary.

On the evening of October 23, 1820, some HBC servants asked to see Simon. When he came out of his house, he saw about thirty men armed with "pikes, guns, swords and pistols." One man tapped him on the shoulder and said, "Je vous prends prisonier de la part du roi" ("I am arresting you in the name of the king"). Simon was seized and "after an arduous struggle" the HBC servants brought him by force into their house. He demanded to see the warrant for his arrest.[10]

The warrant, from a Court of Oyer and Terminer for the district of Montreal, was for the arrest of William McGillivray, Simon McGillivray, and Archibald Norman McLeod. At that point, Simon told them to put away their warrant because the Simon McGillivray named was obviously his uncle. George Simpson, under whose orders Simon had been arrested, at length admitted that was true; however, he refused to release Simon. "I take the responsibility of this measure myself. It is in retaliation for Colin Robertson," he told Simon.[11]

Simon was locked up in the middle of three rooms in a small building with the windows barred with iron. In his diary, he complained bitterly about his treatment. He said that the men residing in the rooms on either side of him behaved with "such indecency and ribaldry . . . as tormented the peace of my mind very much indeed." Also, when he went out "to attend the cravings of nature," he was followed closely by "my keeper with a pair of pistols and a sword."[12]

The day after his arrest, Simon asked to be allowed out on bail and promised that he would appear in Canada to answer any charges that might be preferred against him. Simpson said he would approve bail only if Simon would leave the required amount in specie (coin) with him. Simon replied that because he was not a partner, he did not have access to any specie. As a result, Simpson kept him locked up.

A few days later, Simon's wife, Teresa, and two small children were sent to reside with him. On November 13, Simon wrote that his son, Edward, told him that the cook (a black man named Glasgow) had hit him. Ten days later, Teresa complained that the cook attacked their daughter and that his foot "was imprinted in" her face. Simon immediately sent a note to Simpson, who came with a witness who claimed that the cook accidentally tripped the little girl.[13] Understandably, this did not stop Simon from worrying about his children. In late November, he wrote, "The people of the fort have so much frightened my boy Edward about killing me, that he got up in his sleep about 7 PM and calling out violently, 'They have killed my father. There he lies,' pointing to where his little sister slept."[14]

Apparently in an attempt to protect his family, Simon escaped on December 3, leaving his wife and children behind. He was quite certain that they would be released and allowed to return home once he was gone, which proved to be the case. Simon was next heard of on March 12, 1821, when he signed his diary and asked that it be put in the hands of an unknown man in Montreal.

—≡:≡—

AN AD HEADED "Dog Stolen" in the February 4, 1818, issue of a Montreal newspaper offered an interesting sidelight on William McGillivray's domestic life. The ad read:

Lost or stolen about the 3d instant, a large Newfoundland dog, brown colour and white face, Had a black leather collar about his neck, from which a plate with the owner's name had been torn. The dog is young and apt to follow any person making [much] of him. Whoever will bring the said dog to the office of this newspaper, or to the subscriber, shall receive eight dollars reward. In failure of which, whoever he may be found with shall be prosecuted. Signed W. McGillivray[15]

There is no report whether the dog was ever returned or if it found its way home.

In other family matters, in late August 1819, Susan McGillivray died at Fort William. It seems probable that William and both his sons were in Fort William at the time of Susan's death. Joseph had been at Fort Okanogan (in what is now Washington State) from 1813 until 1817, when he went to Fort William.

In the fall of 1819, McGillivray sailed for Britain aboard the fur-trade ship *Ewerta*. It was his first trip overseas since 1812. It was not a happy visit because of the deaths of four family members, including three of Simon McTavish's children and William's sister Margery Shaw.

The deaths of Alexander Mackenzie and Lord Selkirk occurred in the spring of 1820. Although McGillivray and Mackenzie apparently never reconciled, McGillivray likely felt some sadness to hear that his old friend was dead. Selkirk's death may also have caused him concern because the NWC suit against Selkirk for conspiracy to ruin their trade was still outstanding at the time. Selkirk's death meant that the suit could fail or would at least be delayed. The company desperately needed the money they had hoped to win from Selkirk in order to continue to operate.

Despite all his business worries, it appears that McGillivray was still a well-respected and prominent figure in the Montreal social scene. Dr. John J. Bigsby, who lived in Canada for nearly ten years beginning in 1818, wrote a glowing account of the city of Montreal and its people. He described Montreal as "a stirring and opulent town" with an "enterprising and active" population of more than 50,000 inhabitants. He was particularly impressed with the stone quays lining the St. Lawrence.

Bigsby was surprised to find Montreal society "a pleasing transcript of the best form of London life" and concluded that "few places have so advanced in all the luxuries and comforts of high civilization as Montreal."[16] He was a guest at a dinner party at McGillivray's home, likely following McGillivray's return from England in 1820, and wrote a highly flattering description of him. McGillivray often entertained the political elite, and Bigsby said that he was "well entitled" to such honour not only on the basis of his wealth "but from his popularity, honesty of purpose, and intimate acquaintance with the true interests of the colony." Guests at the dinner attended by Bigsby included a judge or two, some members of the legislative council, and three or four retired partners of the NWC. Food and wine "were perfect" and conversation was "fluent and sensible." Bigsby was seated at the table between one of McGillivray's "two agreeable and well-educated daughters" and explorer David Thompson.[17] After dinner, the guests were entertained by a man singing "Le premier jour de Mai," a voyageur song, and one of McGillivray's daughters, who played the piano. The dinner described by Bigsby may have been the last large social event McGillivray hosted.

16 AMALGAMATION, 1820—21

My summer wife is buried now outside these fortress walls
My sons inscribe her headstone with a tribute to them all
"The mother of the country, the daughter of the land"
We leave you poor with beggar's hands . . .

In London town the deal was signed in 1821
The Hudson's Bay Company had finally won
The Ojibwa chiefs and all the tribes marched into the Great Hall
And hunger and death were the black bird's call . . .
In the big lonely.

RODNEY BROWN, FROM "THE BIG LONELY"[1]

Although William McGillivray realized that the NWC faced serious difficulties when he convened the 1820 rendezvous, no one knew at that time that the final Fort William rendezvous would take place the following year. On July 15, 1820, McGillivray wrote to John George McTavish informing him of his transfer to Fort William to replace Dr. John McLoughlin. McGillivray, like his brother Simon, did not have a very high opinion of McLoughlin. He told McTavish that the doctor, "who feels very sore at being removed from his place," tried every means to defeat the plan. McLoughlin and Angus Bethune had been appointed as deputies to negotiate the new wintering partners' agreement with McTavish & McGillivrays. "The wintering partners here must not consider themselves entirely the NWC," McGillivray warned. The letter to McTavish ended with the postscript, "You should write to your friends in the interior in any way you like to send you powers of attorney next year to act for them. We are likely not to be unanimous in making a new agreement. The people here are a strange set."[2]

The British colonial secretary, Lord Bathurst, appealed to Edward Ellice in 1820 in hopes that he might bring about a union of the HBC and NWC interests. The HBC was in a strong position in subsequent negotiations. They must have been aware that eighteen out of twenty wintering partners at the 1820 NWC rendezvous had authorized John McLoughlin and Angus Bethune to negotiate with the HBC on their behalf. As a result, the HBC could play the wintering partners off against the agents. Even though Bethune and McLoughlin did not directly participate in the subsequent negotiations, they likely still influenced the outcome in a way unfavourable to the NWC. McLoughlin was ill and later insisted that he had been deliberately shut out of the negotiations. Andrew Colvile of the HBC believed that without pressure from the wintering partners the NWC would never have come to terms. Simon McGillivray was critical of the presence of McLoughlin and Bethune; he believed that the the Nor'Westers had been on the verge of a favourable agreement when McLoughlin and Bethune arrived in London.

By the fall of 1820, William McGillivray was extremely concerned about the financial health of both the NWC and McTavish, McGillivrays & Co. He hoped to negotiate a new agreement with the winterers by the time the current McTavish, McGillivrays & Co. agreement ended in two years' time. By then, he thought, surely the case against Selkirk's estate would be settled and damages awarded to the NWC. Also, after eight failed NWC attempts to gain access to Hudson Bay, McGillivray felt that sooner or later they would succeed in having the HBC charter annulled.

The need for more capital for the NWC was becoming critical. Many winterers and even some partners in McTavish, McGillivrays & Co. were threatening to withdraw their money. During McGillivray's trip to London in the winter of 1819–20, he had hesitated to confide the NWC's financial needs to Edward Ellice and his London firm, which had a long connection with the company. In October 1820, however, William wrote to Simon, "It would appear evident that our concern cannot go on without extreme hazard, if at all, unless we have additional capital . . . Every other consideration than that of supporting the concern must . . . be lost sight of." Under the circumstances, Simon would certainly have to approach Edward Ellice for a loan. William ended the letter by saying, "I am, thank God in good health. For two or three weeks after my return [from London in spring 1820] I was most uncomfortable after a bad trip in rainy weather down the Ottawa River, and you know it requires some time to set me to rights."[3]

Colin Robertson met Simon shortly before they both left for England and wrote of the meeting:

> *You must not set me down as a McGillivray man . . . when I confess candidly that I like Simon much better than his friend the Member of Parliament [Ellice]; there is a sort of Highland pride and frankness about the little fellow that I don't dislike. He has no blarney about him . . . He seems bent on a union, and after all his claims and advantages are thrown out, he comes back to that point, and dwells upon it with more than ordinary pleasure.*[4]

Because of William McGillivray's poor health, the thought of travelling to Britain again in the fall of 1820 was not a welcome one; however, as the winter of 1820–21 went on, he began to be increasingly nervous about the state of negotiations in London. He would have no news about what was happening until the first ship of the season arrived in the spring. Because Simon was nineteen years younger than William and had no practical fur-trade experience, William may have thought that Simon was not up to the job of negotiations, despite being a successful businessman. He may also have felt that Simon did not share his own emotional attachment to the NWC.

Finally, a large packet of letters and other documents arrived from England for William. The news was not good. Parliament had not annulled the HBC charter, and Edward Ellice had not agreed to lend the NWC money. Enclosed was a document or indenture of an agreement between the HBC and the NWC dated March 26, 1821. Simon and Ellice had already signed it. Even a cursory look at this document told William that his worst fears regarding the future of the NWC had come to pass. The NWC was to be swallowed up by the HBC and would completely lose its identity. Item No. 4 stated, "That trade heretofore carried on by both parties shall for 21 years ... be carried on by and in the name of the Gov. & Co. exclusively." And in Item No. 19 it was stipulated that "On or previous to 31st December 1822, notice in writing of all the depots, stations &c of the N.W. Co. be given to the Gov. & Co. and possession thereof delivered."[5]

Simon sent William a complete account of what had happened. He and "my friend Mr. Ellice" had begun three months of negotiations with the HBC in December. McLoughlin and Bethune had approached Andrew Colvile, who was both a member of the HBC committee and Lady Selkirk's brother; however, the HBC declined to negotiate with them. Yet Colvile must have been delighted with McLoughlin and Bethune's visit, which certainly provided evidence of the lack of unity among the NWC's partners. In a letter to Lady Selkirk, Colvile wrote, "Simon pure and I settled it in a quarter of an hour. I think Ellice and he were as much afraid of the deal being off as we were, so it was only who was the boldest bully."[6] It is not known if this letter became public at the time; certainly Colvile would not have wished it to be widely circulated.

Despite the fact that William McGillivray was not present during the negotiations, an extract from the HBC minute book of March 21, 1821, makes it sound as if he were there:

> *Resolved that this meeting do sanction the Board of Directors in agreeing to the arrangements proposed to be entered into between this Company and Mr. William McGillivray, Mr. Simon McGillivray and Mr. Edward Ellice on behalf of themselves and the NWC of Montreal, and do fully authorize the Committee to carry the same into effect.*[7]

Several months after William's death, Simon admitted to the NWC creditors that he had actually signed the 1821 agreement between the NWC and the HBC on his own authority:

> *In these arrangements I had neither authority, nor instructions, nor assistance from the NWC, or from McTavish, McGillivrays & Co. . . . I negotiated arrangements and . . . executed deeds*

in my own name and right, and on my own responsibility . . . I had not even a power of attorney from my brother, although for him I had entered into stipulations; and the Company had no security beyond my personal engagement that the arrangement should be carried into effect. I had, indeed, a moral confidence that whatever I did, my brother would support; and that our united influence would carry through any measure . . . but . . . I must declare the arrangements were mine, and he merely aided me in carrying them into effect.[8]

There are no extant documents indicating that William felt Simon had betrayed him by accepting terms of union with the HBC similar to those that William and John Richardson had refused in 1815 when Selkirk first offered them. All of William's public utterances in the following months supported the actions of Simon and Ellice. It seems probable, however, that William—despite realizing that Simon had little choice but to sign the agreement—was devastated by the outcome of the negotiations.

According to a later story, each generation of the descendants of William and Magdalen was formally introduced to the portraits of William with the words, "This one made the fortune," said while pointing at William, and "That one lost it," said while pointing at Simon's likeness.[9] However, this anecdote is almost certainly apocryphal, considering the great pride the McGillivrays took in their family.

In late May, William wrote to Ellice:

The situation of the concerns which for so long a period of my life have been the object of my pursuit are so completely altered that it will take some time to reconcile me to the new order of things and to the sacrifice of objects to which I have all along attached a considerable degree of importance. Circumstances I am aware rendered sacrifices unavoidable and I am ready to acknowledge and fully appreciate the ability [with] which these important negotiations were conducted by yourself and my brother. But concessions have been made which I fear will involve us in much difficulty in carrying the arrangements into effect and in the sequel be found injurious to the trade.[10]

McGillivray disapproved of the exclusion of certain winterers, including Samuel Black and Cuthbert Grant, from the new company and stated that he hoped these men would later have an option to rejoin the company. He admitted that he did not know if they would accept such an offer, but "it would at all events be soothing to their feelings."[11] In fact, both Black and Grant were later reinstated.

All of the other partners in McTavish, McGillivrays & Co. were equally unhappy about the agreement signed by Simon and Ellice. Both Archibald Norman McLeod and Angus Shaw decided to retire. Henry McKenzie, who was married to Angus Bethune's sister, was especially critical of the McGillivrays and withdrew from the company. He later launched a lawsuit against them. Only Thomas Thain, though bitter and protesting Simon's assumption of power of attorney in the matter, remained with McTavish, McGillivrays & Co.

Nicholas Garry and Simon McGillivray, representing the HBC and the NWC respectively, were appointed to put the agreement in place in North America. Although William had described the choice of Garry as "fortunate" in his letter to Ellice, he soon changed his mind when he learned that Garry had crossed the Atlantic with McLoughlin and Bethune rather than with Simon.

On June 7, William, Simon, and Garry left Lachine for Fort William, where they would meet with the wintering partners at the final NWC rendezvous. The winterers listened silently to William's report on the terms of the agreement signed by the two companies, then burst into shouts of indignation. They feared many would be left unemployed, and they wondered how those who didn't lose their jobs would be able to work with their former enemies. "Amalgamation, this is not amalgamation. This is submersion. We are drowned men!" one winterer said bitterly.[12] Finally, they realized the price they were paying for their strong individuality and that had they remained united, they might have won much better terms during the negotiations leading up to the amalgamation.

Robertson wrote about the final Fort William rendezvous as though he had been an eyewitness, but it seems unlikely that he was there. He said that McLoughlin was the only Nor'Wester "who has a grain of real independence in their whole composition [and that] . . . Simon McGillivray has carried everything without even the semblance of opposition." According to Robertson, Simon opened the business on the first day of the rendezvous, on the second day the Deed and Release was signed, and on the third all was peace and harmony. The only exception was that poor Bethune "was sent to Coventry the day after his arrival." Robertson claimed that the wintering partners were not dissatisfied with the union because "any terms would have been acceptable in the present state of their affairs." The half shares given to some partners caused "a little murmur" which Simon McGillivray "smoothed down by a handsome dagger to one, a pair of pistols to another, and a bountiful shower of promises for the vacant factories."[13] Perhaps Robertson really believed that was true, but it is more likely that he chose not to acknowledge how angry the Nor'Westers really were.

The final meeting between the local Ojibwa people and the NWC took place on Saturday, July 7. Two chiefs entered the great hall, preceded by the Union Jack and accompanied by all their people. They sat down and commenced smoking. Then they presented twenty beaver pelts to William McGillivray, "their great father," before one of the chiefs rose and "in a very graceful manner" made a speech. He said that he had only brought a few people with him because they had recently been afflicted with the measles, "but there was another cause, which he even more regretted, which was that a black bird had decoyed away some of his followers."[14]

McGillivray replied that he was happy that they had fulfilled their promise to pay their debts. On the other hand, he regretted that so many were ill and that the black bird (the Americans) had decoyed away some of the people. He said that the NWC and the HBC would become one company but that this would not alter their dealings with the Ojibwa. After his speech, McGillivray presented the two chiefs each with a red coat faced with blue and gold braid, a round hat, and a shirt. "These they put on, undressing in the most formal way without changing a muscle of their countenance." Rum and tobacco "in considerable quantity" was divided among the whole assembly and they smoked the pipe again. Then they departed until the following day when they staged a war dance.[15]

Following the rendezvous, William returned home to Montreal while Garry and Simon McGillivray set out for York Factory. They visited all the NWC posts along the way to inform employees about the amalgamation and to make any needed practical decisions. Garry, who kept a detailed diary of his trip, wrote that when he first met McGillivray, "a simultaneous movement brought our hands together, and if the feeling was not a true one, an intention to act fairly, kindly, considerately by each other, there is more hypocrisy in the world than appears to me to be possible."[16] Sadly, this good feeling did not last very long. At the end of three weeks of meetings in Fort William, Garry wrote that "never in my life have I left a place with less regret."[17]

In early August, Simon McGillivray and Garry arrived at Bas de la Rivière on Lake Winnipeg. The next day, "being anxious on many accounts" not to arrive at the Red River with McGillivray, Garry ordered his canoe to set off at 6 AM, feeling "much relief" in being without his travel companion.[18]

A few days later, Garry arrived at the camp of Ojibwa (Saulteaux) chief Peguis. Because Peguis and his people had offered help to the settlers at the time of the Battle of Seven Oaks, McGillivray refused to stop there. Selkirk had presented Peguis with a Union Jack with the HBC arms on it, and Peguis now had the flag raised over his camp in honour of Garry's visit. He also showed Garry a testimonial from Selkirk written on moosehide saying that Peguis had always been a faithful, sincere friend of the colony and recommending him to the attentions of the officers of the HBC.[19]

On another day, Garry's canoe got caught in a storm on Lake Winnipeg and scarcely made it safely to shore. After he landed, Garry saw that Simon was still out on the lake and did not seek shelter until the storm became even worse. While Garry admitted that Simon's canoe was larger than his and could better stand the high waves, he still criticized McGillivray's behaviour:

> We learnt afterwards that the standing out was only bravado, wishing us first to encamp that they might have the opportunity to vaunt their prowess. Miserable vanity, which might have cost the lives of many brave people, who protested against the step. The steersman was actually changed [for] refusing to conduct the canoe. The history of his vanity was that after an attempt at Fort William to give me a weak crew and a bad canoe, it was a source of great annoyance that we led the march.[20]

At Norway House on August 11, Garry presided over the first meeting of the Council of the Northern Department, which endorsed the appointments made at Fort William and formally abandoned the Montreal–Fort

William supply route—despite Simon's strong objections—in favour of the route through York Factory.

On August 23, Garry and Simon McGillivray arrived at York Factory shortly after two ships from England. One ship contained 170 colonists from Switzerland. Garry charged that two Canadians from Simon's canoe "were poisoning the minds" of the new colonists. Both Garry and the HBC governor ordered the two men out of the camp, but they refused to go, saying that Garry was not their bourgeois. Garry consulted with McGillivray, asking him to discipline the men, but "instead of at once ordering them off, he reasoned with them and even took their part."[21]

On September 14, 1821, Garry set sail on *Prince of Wales* to return to England. As he left, he said that he thought "My mission brought to bear fruit, all parties satisfied and united except those who have sinister and sordid views to carry into effect (which I have had the advantage to unmask) and having had it in my power to protect so many people who otherwise would have suffered."[22] What Simon McGillivray thought of the trip is unknown.

George Simpson, who would later become governor of the HBC, met with Garry at Norway House. Both Garry and Simpson displayed an extreme bias against Simon McGillivray. Simpson gave Garry credit for "kind, polite and conciliatory measures" by which "he effectually removed all party feeling, jealousy and discontents; our old opponents no longer viewed us as enemies but met us as acquaintances which I think will soon assume the character of friendship." McGillivray's behaviour was just the opposite, Simpson charged. The result was "to excite a general personal regard and respect" for Garry while McGillivray "was despised and this feeling was as prevalent among our fresh allies as our own party."[23]

Simpson went on to say that Garry "had to deal with a deep designing and I may add dishonourable people," but that his good management "rendered them unavailing." McGillivray, he charged, "to gain his own selfish ends, sacrificed the interests of the Company." However, by depending too much on his cunning, he overreached himself and put Garry on his guard. Thus, Garry foiled McGillivray at all points.[24]

Simpson, who realized that McGillivray had a grudge against him for having arrested Simon McGillivray Jr. in Athabasca, was not willing to admit any fault in that matter. He wrote, "The circumstances are fully and carefully explained in my journal and I am not inclined to admit that I was not justified in every part of my conduct throughout the campaign."[25]

⸙

FOLLOWING HIS FINAL trip to Fort William with Simon and Nicholas Garry, William McGillivray was a defeated and depressed man who may indeed have felt that his life's work had been destroyed. He might have fought harder to play a significant role in the new company, but his poor health made that impossible. Because of Simon's role in negotiations, William put the best possible face on matters in a letter to his old friend John Strachan, dated July 26, 1821, from Fort William:

> *These arrangements are happily completed, and I part with my old troops, to meet them no more in discussion on the Indian trade; this parting I confess does not cause me much regret. I have worked hard and honestly for them, and I am satisfied that I have, at least, done my duty . . . Thus the fur trade is forever lost to Canada! The Treaty of Ghent destroyed the southern trade. Still the capital and exertions of a few individuals supported the Northern trade under many disadvantages against a chartered company, who brought their goods to the Indian Country at less than one half the expense that ours cost us—but it would have been worse than folly to have continued the contest further. We have made no submission. We met and negotiated on equal terms.[26]*

McGillivray went on to explain how the new organization would work. The HBC and the agents from McTavish, McGillivrays & Co. were each given thirty shares in the new concern. Forty other shares were divided among the wintering partners—twenty-five to former Nor'Westers and fifteen to HBC men. The board of directors for the new company, which would sit in London, was composed of two members of the HBC committee and two NWC members plus the governor and deputy governor. He expected that "until the country is got into proper order it is probable I must assume charge of it, which for some little time will occasion my absence from Canada."[27]

McGillivray concluded his letter by commenting on the loss of trade to Montreal. "The loss of this trade to Montreal . . . will be severely felt . . . The yearly disbursements in cash from the office in Montreal . . . was not less than £40,000 per annum . . . and combined with the present distressed state of the trade in the province is a matter of regret."[28]

Although McGillivray optimistically told his friend Strachan that he expected to play an important role in the new company, this did not happen. While he spent most of the next two years in London, McGillivray did only minimal work during that time. For all practical purposes, his fur-trade days were over.

17 WINDING DOWN, 1822–25

The Isle of Mull is of isles the fairest
Of ocean's gems 'tis the first and rarest,
Green grassy island of sparkling fountains,
Of waving woods and high tow'ring mountains.

. . .

But gone are now all those joys for ever,
Like bubbles bursting on yonder river
Farewell, farewell, to thy sparkling fountains,
Thy waving woods and high tow'ring mountains.

MALCOLM MacFARLANE
FROM "AN-T-EILEAN MUILEACH" (THE ISLE OF MULL)

In the fall of 1821, William McGillivray travelled to London with his daughters, sixteen-year-old Anne and thirteen-year-old Magdalen, and spent almost two years there before returning to Montreal. His son Simon, who was close to his two half-sisters and would later name one of his daughters Anne, spent the winter of 1822–23 with them. At that time, Joseph was in either Norway House or York Factory as a chief trader, and William's other daughter, Elizabeth, was likely in Quebec with her husband. Many suitors courted Anne that winter. Thomas Richardson Auldjo was the most persistent, and he and Anne married in

1826 when she was 21. Auldjo was a nephew of McGillivray's colleague John Richardson, and his mother was a first cousin to Edward Ellice.

In the spring of 1823, McGillivray wrote to John George McTavish of his concerns about his son Simon and the new HBC governor George Simpson. Although McGillivray considered Simpson an able business man, he knew him to have little respect for Native women. Simpson once wrote to a colleague asking that he take care of a woman that Simpson no longer wished to be bothered with, saying, "If you can dispose of the lady it will be satisfactory to me as she is an unnecessary and expensive appendage."[1] McGillivray undoubtedly feared that Simon would quarrel with Simpson if he made slighting remarks about Simon's wife, Teresa. He wrote:

> *Simon left us last week . . . [with] the March packet for New York. His trip to this country I have no doubt has done him much good. The unfortunate self-sufficiency that a young man who has no previous character formed acquires in the North West plays much against himself and is troublesome to those who wish him well . . . Both his uncle and myself have had serious talks with him regarding his quarrel with Mr. Simpson, and we have had some trouble to drive savage ideas from him. But he has promised to think no more of it . . . I rather think Mr. Simpson will feel inclined to make things pleasant for him.*[2]

It is not clear whether McGillivray personally felt that offspring from country marriages should be considered legitimate and able to inherit in the same way as their legitimate half-siblings; however, back on March 14, 1818, McGillivray had written to William Coltman, the commissioner who investigated the events at Seven Oaks regarding the Métis:

> *Many were linked to the NWC from the ties of consanguinity and interest . . . yet they one and all look upon themselves as members of an independent tribe of natives, entitled to a property in the soil, to a flag of their own, and to protection from the British Government . . . It is absurd to consider them legally in any other light than as Indians; the British law admits of no filiation of*

illegitimate children but that of the mother; and as these persons
cannot in law claim any advantage by paternal right, it follows
that they ought not to be subjected to any disadvantages which
might be supposed to arise from the fortuitous circumstances of
their parentage.[3]

⇒:⇐

IN 1822, HBC Governor George Simpson presided over his first
annual meeting at York Factory. Trader John Tod described a formal banquet held at the gathering. It was the first social meeting of
the superior officers, and seventy-three men were present. Tod set the
stage by commenting that the banquet had some peculiar features,
owing to the bitter feelings of guests who had been keen trade competitors and often personal antagonists for many years. The men met
in the great mess hall, which was three hundred feet long, and were
seated at two long tables.

> *The former Nor'Westers—mostly Highland men—had been*
> *stalking about the old fort as haughtily as had been their wont at*
> *their own former headquarters . . . not trying to converse with*
> *the Hudson's Bay men. It was dollars to doughnuts . . . whether*
> *the entertainment would be a feed or a fight . . . [The two groups]*
> *entered the great hall in silence, and kept wholly apart until*
> *the new governor moving in the throng with bows, smiles and*
> *introductions brought about some conversation or hand-shaking*
> *between individuals.*[4]

Finally, Simpson pointed politely at the places where he wished each
guest to sit. Men who had lately slashed at each other with swords and still
bore marks of the combat found themselves glaring at each other across
the narrow banquet table. Two such men had fought a pistol duel across a
campfire one night, and another pair were former jailer and prisoner. Tod
concluded that the situation was saved by the example of demonstrative,
if rather insincere, comradeship shown by several superior officers who
were also former rivals. As well, "the good effects of the fine wine used so
lavishly . . . cannot be denied."[5]

It would be interesting to know how William McGillivray would have rated the York Factory banquet compared to the lavish feasts he had hosted at Fort William. While no mention of his sons was made, it is possible that one or both of them could have been in attendance and reported back to him.

—≡:≡—

AFTER AMALGAMATION, CUTHBERT Grant was one of only two or three Nor'Westers "of significance" who were excluded from employment with the new company. Simpson, who met Grant in February 1822, described him as "a very steady good tempered and well behaved man" who was "entirely made a party tool . . . in the late unfortunate business." Simpson decided that Grant could become "a most useful man by good management"; but if treated harshly, he could become "a most dangerous enemy." Simpson decided to use "good management," and Grant was reinstated as a fur trader.[6]

At this time, William McGillivray still controlled the legacy Grant had received from his father. Simpson learned this fact and went about ingratiating himself with Grant. Grant showed Simpson a letter from McGillivray recommending he go to Canada to get clear of the Bills of Indictment. Grant planned to do so in the spring and then also go to England to look into his private affairs. McGillivray had acknowledged holding the sum of four or five thousand pounds from the estate of Cuthbert Grant Sr., but Grant told Simpson that he was quite certain the amount should be almost ten thousand pounds more than that.

Although Grant did go to Montreal, he was never brought to trial. Nothing is known about his trip to England, if in fact he did make one. On May 31, 1824, Simpson wrote to Colvile of the HBC in London that he had received an order to transfer Grant's money into the hands of the Company. Grant had, according to Simpson, "made me his trustee and executor, and put his affairs principally under my management."[7]

—≡:≡—

McGILLIVRAY WROTE OPTIMISTICALLY to John George McTavish in March 1822 regarding the first joint financial report between the amalgamated companies. He claimed credit for much of its success.

*The despatch from the governor and committee has been framed
. . . from the best suggestions and information which I could
give, and I must say that they were received in the best manner
. . . if the council will follow the matter up and look only to the
company's interest, which is their own, of course, I have sanguine
hopes of success.*[8]

A few months later, however, McGillivray had changed his tune. In a
second letter to McTavish, he said that the beaver market was falling. As
a result, in order to avoid a heavy loss on the furs shipped from Montreal
by the NWC in 1820, the greater part still remained on hand, including
"28,000 skins beaver and almost all the muskrats and foxes." The shipment from the Columbia fortunately was disposed of at Canton at $4.75
per skin. "But altogether the affairs of 1819, 1820 and 1821 must turn
out very bad."[9]

The attitude of the governor and committee of the HBC toward
William McGillivray and his fellow Nor'Westers can be summed up
in an official letter (date unknown) sent by the committee to George
Simpson, which stated, "We consider that you have acquired a more
perfect knowledge of the Indian trade than perhaps was ever possessed by any one individual, or even by any body of men who have
been engaged in it."[10] It is shocking that the governor and committee so
completely ignored the many skilled traders connected with the NWC
over the years, no matter how highly they rated Simpson's ability. This
statement clearly shows the utter lack of respect that the HBC had for
former Nor'Westers.

Although the 1821 HBC agreement was supposed to run for twenty-
one years, it was completely revised three years later. By the new agreement,
the McGillivrays and Ellice were given substantial blocks of stock in lieu
of shares of profit. In addition, the joint advisory board was phased out
with the result that the McGillivrays became merely private shareholders
who had no further influence in running the HBC. According to historian W. Stewart Wallace, the joint board had been set up in 1821 "partly
no doubt in order to spare the feelings of the McGillivrays and partly in
order to ensure the smooth absorption of the Nor'Westers into the HBC.
By 1824, thanks to the wise measures of George Simpson . . . the second
of these objects had been achieved."[11]

The new agreement also stipulated that the three men were required to set aside, out of the stocks allotted to them, shares to the amount of fifty thousand pounds to meet any claims against either the NWC or McTavish, McGillivrays & Co. The original partnership between the NWC and the HBC ended formally on September 15, 1824. On November 24, Edward Ellice took an oath of fidelity to the Governor and Company of Adventurers of England and became a member of the committee. Simon did not take the oath, but it is unknown whether he declined to do so or simply was not asked.

As a result of the provision in the 1824 agreement that the McGillivrays and Ellice set aside shares to meet claims against them, Simon McGillivray was forced to sell his valuable collection of paintings at auction. A two-day sale of his art collection was held in May 1825, conducted by Christie's in London. His collection was so large that the sale catalogue ran to sixteen pages; it included paintings by well-known artists such as Titian, Rembrandt, Rubens, Watteau, van Eyck, and Murillo.[12]

In August 1825, Thomas Thain, who was in charge of the Montreal offices of McTavish, McGillivrays & Co., as well as resident agent of the HBC for the Montreal district, suddenly left for London. Shortly after his arrival in London, he was removed to an insane asylum.

⸻

McGILLIVRAY'S FIFTY-EIGHTH BIRTHDAY took place in the spring of 1823, about the time that his son Simon returned to North America. William and his daughters likely visited his Scottish estate of Pennyghael on the Isle of Mull during the summer. Later that fall, they returned to Montreal where, on October 6, he was installed as the Provincial Grand Master of the Free and Accepted Masons of England for the District of Montreal and the Borough of William Henry. Also that fall, Alexander Henry died at the age of eighty-five.

The following summer, McGillivray's health began to decline and he made a new will. To Anne and Magdalen, he left the income from his estate on Mull, marriage settlements of ten thousand pounds each, and "the trinkets and jewels [that] belong to their late mother."[13] He left Simon and Joseph two thousand pounds each, plus all the lands he possessed in Canada. His son-in-law Daniel Jourdain (husband of his daughter Elizabeth) was relieved of all his debts, and Elizabeth received a legacy. His sister Mary, who had kept house for him since his wife Magdalen's death, received an annuity. He left Pennyghael to his brother Simon since it was entailed in such a way that neither his daughters nor the twins (considered illegitimate) could inherit it. He also left numerous smaller bequests to relatives and friends and to the poor in his native parish of Dunlichity and in Pennyghael.

In 1825, William and Simon petitioned for a family coat of arms as "a lasting memorial of the discoveries made by the North West Company under the direction of . . . William and Simon McGillivray." The coat of arms included the ancient motto of their clan, "Touch not the cat bot a glove."[14]

At the time, McGillivray was depressed due to poor health and business problems. The only bright spot for him that spring and summer was the dedication of the Montreal Masonic Temple, which he attended as Right Worshipful Provincial Grand Master in the Masonic Order for the Montreal district. McGillivray's doctor advised him

William and Simon McGillivray were granted a family coat of arms as "a lasting memorial of the discoveries made by the North West Company" under their direction. HBC ARCHIVES, TRANSPARENCY NO. 16636, REFERENCE/COLLECTION NO. F.6-5

to travel to a milder climate, so he decided to return to London and Scotland in the fall.

On August 4, Simon wrote to Ellice to tell him about the state of his brother's health and of his trip to London. Simon was lobbying for a place for William on the HBC committee. He wrote, "As to the usefulness of his information and experience in the matters to be discussed at the Hudson's Bay House, there can be but one opinion, and I should hope there can be no objection on any side to his being elected a member of the committee." At the same time, however, Simon admitted to Ellice that both Thain and the McGillivrays had badly managed NWC business affairs. "We were all, if you please, but Thain most of any, too careless of money . . . he has given away thousands of which no account can be made."[15]

As one of his last acts, McGillivray wrote a new will that named Simon as his sole executor and general legatee, thereby enabling Simon to immediately apply the money or property he inherited toward paying debts. As a result, none of his children received any of the money he had left to them in his previous will.

William McGillivray died in London on Sunday, October 16, 1825. Edward Ellice was one of the last people to visit him before his death. Soon after, Ellice wrote to Simon:

> You will have heard enough of the sad, sad termination of your poor brother's sufferings without my entering into the painful details. On the Sunday early [the day of his death] I heard of the unfavourable changes [and] . . . I went up to town . . . although too late to be of any use, I had some satisfaction in paying the only respect in my power to his memory . . .
>
> His anxiety to place in your hands every means and assistance in his power to meet a situation which he foresaw would be attended with extreme difficulty and embarrassment and the wisdom and prudence of the last act of his life are so many proofs (if proofs indeed were wanting to those who knew him) of a mind gifted with no ordinary qualities of manliness, integrity and the highest principle.[16]

THE LAST LAIRD OF THE
NORTH WEST COMPANY

Your race was not begotten
Of weeds, nor of worthless grass,
Nor did it grow in the edges of the field,
But sprang from the finest of wheat;
These are the excellent plants
Healthy, erect, pure soft,
Who would raise a banner on its staff
Around Lachlan the Beloved.

. . .

Handsome, excellent gentlemen
Who would not spare themselves in army or camp,
Marching over moss and hill, army or
Wood, and in rough places, hollows and mountains,
Who would not spare their effects
Nor their high precious blood
To avoid danger
That William might never be in difficulty.

JOHN DONN M'JAMES V'DAVID FROM
"SONG TO MacGILLIVRAY OF DUNMAGLASS"

Since before the amalgamation with the HBC in 1821, Simon McGillivray had been working hard to address the serious financial problems the former NWC was undergoing. Two months after William's death, he sent a memorandum to the creditors describing the situation at the time that he and Ellice entered negotiations with the HBC. Although he blamed part of the financial problem on the losses sustained and expenses incurred as a result of the contest against Selkirk and the HBC, he also partially blamed NWC partners. Many of them were without capital and some were deeply indebted to the company. Simon wrote:

> *My brother was considered a man of fortune; and he had been, in fact, originally the only capitalist among us; but his partners also seemed impatient . . . and some of them, who had not brought a shilling of capital into the House, had scarcely got their names admitted into the firm, when they at once launched into all sorts of expenses . . . [In addition, some of the partners were] not only useless, but burthensome to us, and whom yet we feared to cast off because they had the power to injure us.*[1]

Simon admitted that the amalgamation arrangements he negotiated with the HBC had not pleased the NWC partners in general, but he argued that "it was effected just in time to save the whole concern from destruction; and our circumstances not being known to our opponents, and they also having their own reasons for wishing to terminate the contest, I obtained liberal, and even advantageous terms for all parties connected with the NWC."[2]

In January 1826, Simon McGillivray followed up his memorandum to creditors with an explanation of how the NWC had operated over the years. On the termination of the partnership of McTavish, McGillivrays & Co. on November 30, 1822, the McGillivray brothers and Thain had been appointed as agents for the province of Quebec "for superintending and managing therein the trade and concerns" of the HBC. At that time, Simon had to admit to the creditors that the papers connected with the Montreal accounts were locked up in the rooms of Thomas Thain, who was unavailable, but Simon did not admit that he and his brother had been careless in not keeping closer track of Thain's work—an oversight that is apparent in documents from the final years of the NWC. It was not until February 1826 that Thain, who had arrived in London the previous September, finally wrote to the NWC wintering partners. He said that he had been seized "with a most violent attack of brain fever, which brought me so low that my life was considered in very imminent danger. I have since had repeated relapses."[3]

Almost immediately after William's death, Simon had placed the whole of both his and William's personal fortunes at the disposal of their creditors. However, because the creditors were still unsatisfied, Simon was forced to put his affairs into the hands of trustees. This is not surprising given the dire financial situation of both the NWC and the McGillivray family at this time. There is no evidence that either Simon or William was guilty of dishonesty, but they certainly had not managed their financial affairs prudently.

The available evidence does not support Simon's contention that he obtained liberal terms "for all parties connected with the NWC" in his negotiations and that the NWC books were balanced in 1821. Up to 1814, the NWC had been prosperous, but NWC historian W. Stewart Wallace believed that "an accurate accounting" of its operations between 1814 and 1821 would have shown that "it was plunging into bankruptcy." The NWC distributed its profits at the end of each year, rather than keeping a reserve fund; therefore, it "was ill equipped to meet a prolonged struggle such as was imposed on it by Lord Selkirk."[4]

Simon was unable to solve his severe financial problems and finally accepted a position as a gold commissioner in South America in 1829. The next year, trustees for the creditors received £110,000 from Ellice, but this only gave creditors a return of ten shillings on the pound. It was fortunate that Ellice was a wealthy man because the litigation went on for many years. The last claims were not settled until 1851.

≡:≡

IN ADDITION TO the poor financial management practices of the McGillivrays, a number of factors brought about the catastrophic fall of the NWC and the McGillivray family with it. The fur trade, by its very nature, was a risky business. In the 1790s, Alexander Mackenzie described how it took more than three years to make a return on money invested, making it "a very heavy business." Added to this, the ongoing competition between competing companies—the long-term rivalry with the HBC and short-term rivalry with the New NWC or XY Company—plus the China trade created a severe financial strain.

Most disastrous, however, was the conflict between the NWC and Lord Selkirk. Many people at the time were strongly partisan for either the NWC or for Selkirk. From the vantage point of two centuries later, however, it seems fairer to apportion blame to both sides. As Wallace wrote, "Lord Selkirk may deserve the credit for establishing in the Canadian West the first colony of real settlers; but he deserves just as well the opprobrium of having ruined the first great industry that Canadians, by means of fortitude and foresight, had developed."[5] On the other hand, many of the Nor'Westers caused the settlers unnecessary hardship by destroying their homes and crops.

As for William McGillivray himself, all indications are that during his first years in North America he quickly became a skilful fur trader and was an excellent manager during the decade following 1804. After 1815, however, he was much less effective in guiding the company. Like his uncle, Simon McTavish, McGillivray sometimes let nepotism or friendship interfere with good business practices. Even more serious, he was responsible for letting relations with the wintering partners deteriorate so badly that the partners revolted, led by Angus Bethune and John McLoughlin. By the early 1820s, he had lost virtually everything. It is not clear what led to McGillivray's later problems, but it seems it was at least partially due to poor health. There is no way of knowing if the NWC would have achieved a more favourable agreement with the HBC had McGillivray been able to take an active role in negotiations, or if the NWC had not already been in such bad financial straits.

William McGillivray was buried in London's St. James Burial Ground, beside his second wife, Magdalen. A monument in honour of Susan, first wife of William McGillivray, was raised in the Fort William Cemetery at an unknown date, likely by her sons Simon and Joseph. It is inscribed, "To the Memory of Susan the mother of Simon, Joseph, & Peter McGillivray who died 26 August 1819." Strangely, Peter, who died as a young child, is mentioned but Elizabeth, who was still living at the time of her mother's death, is not. A modern memorial dedicated to Susan is located at Mountainview Cemetery in Thunder Bay. The original stone was moved there in 1883 from the Fort William cemetery on the Kaministiquia River.

According to marriage and death records, Susan and William's daughter Elizabeth was married at the age of twenty-one in 1807 to a voyageur named Daniel Jourdain and died in Quebec in 1858 when she was seventy-five. While the dates of her marriage and death are likely correct, she was likely born in 1790 and thus married at the age of seventeen rather than twenty-one. There is only a record of her having one child, a daughter named Genevieve.

In 1821, Joseph McGillivray was promoted to chief trader at Norway House. He retired from the fur trade in 1831 and died the following year in Montreal. He was married to Françoise Roy and had two sons.

Joseph's brother Simon also became a chief trader with the HBC. In 1826, Simpson planned an expedition from the Red River to Snake River country. Cuthbert Grant was nominally in charge of the party, but Simon, who was second-in-command, actually directed the enterprise. Simpson wrote, "Mr. McGillivray's spirit, activity and business-like arrangements render him well-qualified for the conduct of the enterprise."[6] Simon continued to work almost until the time of his death in 1840 at the age of fifty. He was married to Theresa Roy and had nine children with her.

It was not until 1861 that the city finally tore down the ruins of Simon McTavish's house. About a decade later, his mausoleum was destroyed and covered with rubble to deter grave robbers and quell ghost stories about the site. In 2010, archaeologists unearthed the monument, uncovering the words "Sacred to the memory of Simon McTavish Esquire."

Some historians have claimed that when Simon McGillivray Sr. went to South America as a gold commissioner, he left William's two younger daughters in a destitute condition in London. That certainly is overstating the case. Anne had married Thomas Richardson Auldjo, nephew of the wealthy Edward Ellice in 1826. Magdalen lived with Anne and her husband until she married William C.C. Brackenbury, the British vice-consul at Cadiz in 1842. Anne was childless, while Magdalen gave birth to four children. McGillivray biographer Marjorie Wilkins Campbell met some of Magdalen's direct descendants in England and Spain in the late 1950s.[7] There are many direct descendants of William McGillivray and Susan across Canada, including Felix, grandson of the author of this biography.

IN 1836, AMERICAN author Washington Irving wrote a nostalgic epitaph to the NWC fur-trade empire and the enterprising family who built it: "The feudal state of Fort William is at an end; its council chamber is silent and deserted; its banquet hall no longer echoes to the burst of loyalty or the 'auld-world' ditty; the lords of the lakes and forests have passed away; and the hospitable magnates of Montreal where are they?"[8]

Today, William McGillivray, the Laird of Fort William, is remembered and his legacy celebrated at the Fort William Historical Park at Thunder Bay, built near the site of the "feudal state" eulogized by Irving.

⇒ NOTES ⇐

PREFACE
1. Chester Martin, *Lord Selkirk's Work in Canada* (Oxford: Clarendon Press, 1916), http://peel.library.ualberta.ca/, 31.

INTRODUCTION
1. John McTavish, Family Tree Maker's Genealogy website. http://familytreemaker.genealogy.com/wfttop.html.

CHAPTER 1: FAMILY TIES: THE McGILLIVRAYS AND McTAVISHES, 1764–76
1. William Mackay, *Sidelights on Highland History*. Inverness: Northern Counties Newspaper and Print and Publishing Company, 1925. Marjorie Wilkins Campbell fonds (P128), 122–23.

CHAPTER 2: THE BIRTH OF THE NORTH WEST COMPANY, 1774–84
1. W. Stewart Wallace, ed., *Documents Relating to the North West Company* (Toronto: The Champlain Society, 1934), www.champlainsociety.ca/, 47.
2. Ibid., 48.
3. Ibid., 56.
4. Ibid., 58.
5. Henry, Alexander (the Elder). *Travels and Adventures in Canada and the Indian Territories between the Years 1760 and 1776* (New York: I Riley, 1809), www.canadiana.org/, 314.
6. Ibid., 329.
7. Harold A. Innis, *Peter Pond: Fur Trader and Adventurer* (Toronto: Irwin & Gordon, 1930), www.gutenberg.ca, 208.
8. Milo M. Quaife, ed., *The John Askin Papers*, vol. I (Detroit: Detroit Library Commission, 1928–1931), http://quod.lib.umich.edu/, 127.
9. Wallace, *Documents Relating to the North West Company*, 63.
10. Harold A. Innis, *The Fur Trade in Canada*, rev. ed. (Toronto: University of Toronto Press, 1956), 181.
11. Quaife, *The John Askin Papers*, vol. I, 76–77.
12. Innis, *The Fur Trade in Canada*, 182.

CHAPTER 3: A NEW LAND, 1783–84
1. Peter Kalm, *Travels into North America*. vol. 3, translated by John Reinhold Forster (Cambridge: Cambridge University Press, 2011; first published in London by Eyres, 1771), 71.
2. William George Beers quoted in British American Magazine (1863), 472–79, cited in Peter C. Newman, *Caesars of the Wilderness* (Markham: Penguin Books, 1987), 47–48.

3. Isaac Weld, *Travels through the States of North America and the Provinces of Upper and Lower Canada, During the Years 1795, 1796, and 1797* (London: John Stockdale, 1799), http://eco.canadiana.ca/.

4. Ibid., 225–26.

5. Dr. Elinor Kyte Senior, "Christmas Eve in Montreal 1783—A Bleak Mid-Winter." *Loyalist Gazette* 24 (June 1986), http://www.uelac.org/, 1–2.

6. Ibid.

7. Ibid.

8. George Thomas Landmann, *Adventures and Recollections of Colonel Landmann Late of the Corps of Royal Engineers*, vol. 1 (London: Colburn & Co., 1852), http://babel.hathitrust.org/., 220–22.

9. Ibid.

10. Ibid., 226.

11. Ibid., 230.

12. Henry, *Travels and Adventures*, 82.

CHAPTER 4: HEADING FOR LE PAYS D'EN HAUT, 1784

1. Georges Dugas, *Un Voyageur des pays d'en Haut*, translated by Carolyn Podruchny (St. Boniface: Éditions des Plaines, 1981; first published 1890 by C.O. Beauchemin & fils), quoted in Carolyn Podruchny, *Making the Voyageur World: Travelers and Traders in the North American Fur Trade* (Toronto: University of Toronto Press, 2006), 169.

2. Jean Morrison, *Superior Rendezvous-Place: Fort William in the Canadian Fur Trade* (Toronto: National Heritage Books, 2001), 47.

3. Alexander Ross. *The Fur Hunters of the Far West: A Narrative of Adventures in the Oregon and Rocky Mountains*, vol. I (London: Smith, Elder & Co., 1855), http://eco.canadiana.ca/, 303–4.

4. Daniel Williams Harmon, *Sixteen Years in the Indian Country: the Journal of Daniel Williams Harmon*, edited by W. Kaye Lamb (Toronto: Macmillan, 1957), 22.

5. Ross, *The Fur Hunters*, 235–36.

CHAPTER 5: "JE SUIS UN HOMME DU NORD," 1784–94

1. Rodney Brown, *North Land* (Starsilk Records, 2009), compact disc.

2. Charles M. Gates, ed. "The Diary of John MacDonnell," in *Five Fur Traders of the Northwest: Being the Narrative of Peter Pond and the Diaries of John MacDonell, Archibald N. McLeod, Hugh Faries and Thomas Connor,* introduction by Grace Lee Nute (Minneapolis: University of Minnesota Press, 1933), 107, 110.

3. L.R. Masson, ed., "Reminiscences by the Honourable Roderic McKenzie," in *Les Bourgeois de la Compagnie du Nord-Ouest.* vol. 1 (Quebec: A. Coté et Cie., 1889–90), http://archive.org/ 13.

4. Marjorie Wilkins Campbell, *The North West Company*, (Vancouver: Douglas & McIntyre, 1973 [Includes the NWC's view regarding amalgamation with the HBC]), 48.

5. Masson, "Reminiscences by the Honourable Roderic McKenzie," in *Les Bourgeois*, vol. 1, 16.

6. Ibid., 17–18.

7. Marjorie Wilkins Campbell, *McGillivray: Lord of the Northwest* (Toronto: Clarke, Irwin, 1962), 45.

8. Harry W. Duckworth, *The English River Notebook: A North West Company Journal and Account Book of 1786* (Montreal: McGill-Queen's University Press, 1990), 136.

9. Campbell, *McGillivray*, 48.

10. Ibid., 66.

11. Morrison, *Superior Rendezvous-Place*, 41.

12. Campbell, *McGillivray*, 49.

13. Ibid.

14. Ibid.

15. Jean Morrison, "Some Fur Trade Families from Lake Superior to Rainy Lake," in *Lake Superior to Rainy Lake: Three Centuries of Fur Trade History,* edited by Jean Morrison (Thunder Bay: Thunder Bay Historical Museum Society, 2003), 103.

16. Duncan McGillivray, *The Journal of Duncan M'Gillivray of the North West Company at Fort George on the Saskatchewan, 1794-5*, edited by A.S. Morton (Toronto: Macmillan, 1929), http://peel.library.ualberta.ca/, 11–12.

17. Duncan McGillivray, *The Journal of Duncan M'Gillivray*, 12.

18. For more details about the South Branch Massacre, see Irene Ternier Gordon, *People of the Fur Trade: From Native Trappers to Chief Factors* (Victoria: Heritage House, 2011), 72–73.

19. Duncan McGillivray, *The Journal of Duncan M'Gillivray*, 25–26.

20. Ibid., 30–32.

21. Ibid., 36.

22. Ibid., 45.

23. Ibid., 46.

24. Ibid., 47.

25. Ibid., 73.

CHAPTER 6: MONTREAL: BUILDING THE NORTH WEST COMPANY, 1784–94

1. Wallace, *Documents Relating to the North West Company*, 75.

2. Ibid., 76–77.

3. Fernand Ouellet , "Frobisher, Joseph," *DCBO*, vol. 5, accessed June 18, 2013, www.biographi.ca/en/bio/frobisher_joseph_5E.html.

4. Ibid.

5. Ouellet , "Frobisher, Joseph," *DCBO*.

6. Ibid.

7. Elaine Allan Mitchell, "The North West Company Agreement of 1795," *Canadian Historical Review* 36, no. 2 (June 1955): 128–29.

8. Ibid., 129–30.

9. Larry Gingras, *The Beaver Club Jewels* (Canadian Numismatic Research Society, 1972), Beaver Club Collection (P305), McCord Museum, 8.

10. Wallace, *Documents Relating to the North West Company*, 138.

11. Gingras, *The Beaver Club Jewels*, 8.

12. *The Beaver Club Minute Book*, Beaver Club fonds (P305), McCord Museum.

13. Ibid.

CHAPTER 7: ROCKY NOR'WESTER RELATIONS, 1793–97

1. Rodney Brown, *The Big Lonely* (Starsilk Records, 2004), compact disc.

2. Mary Quayle Innis, ed., *Mrs. Simcoe's Diary* (Toronto: Macmillan, 1965), 65.

3. Alexander Mackenzie, *Voyages from Montreal on the River St. Laurence through the Continent of North America*. London: T. Cadell, 1801. http://peel.library.ualberta.ca/, 28–30.

4. Michael Brown, ed., "Transnational Dimensions," in *Layers of Power: Societies and Institutions in Europe*, edited by Saúl Martínez Bermejo (Pisa: Pisa University Press, 2010), http://ehlee.humnet.unipi.it/books5/1/06.pdf, 238.

5. Ibid.

6. Ibid., 239.

7. *North West Company Letter Books*, 1792–1824. North West Company Collection (C104) and Marjorie Wilkins Campbell fonds (P128), McCord Museum.

8. Letter, James Hallowell to Simon McTavish, November 17, 1794, F.3/1 fol. 208, HBC Archives.

9. Campbell, *McGillivray*, 79–80.

10. Ibid., 80.

11. Masson, *Les Bourgeois de la Compagnie du Nord-Ouest*. vol. 1 (Quebec: A. Coté et Cie., 1889–90), http://archive.org/, 44.

12. For the text of the 1795 agreement, see Mitchell, "The North West Company Agreement of 1795," 135–45.

13. Article III. "Primary Documents in American History: Jay's Treaty." Library of Congress, http://www.loc.gov/rr/program/bib/ourdocs/jay.html, 117.

14. Landmann, *Adventures and Recollections*, 232.

15. Ibid., 234.

16. Ibid., 295. A "deoch an dorus" is a farewell drink at the door.

17. Landmann, *Adventures and Recollections*, 301.

CHAPTER 8: VIOLENCE AND THE NEW NORTH WEST COMPANY, 1798–1806

1. Podruchny, *Making the Voyageur World*, 74.

2. Jean Morrison, "MacKay, Alexander," in DCBO, vol. 5, accessed June 18, 2013, www. biographi.ca/en/bio/mackay_alexander_5E.html; Wallace, *Documents Relating to the North West Company*, 221–22.

3. Gordon Charles Davidson, *The North West Company* (Berkeley: University of California Press, 1918), 91.

4. E.E. Rich, *The Fur Trade and the Northwest to 1857* (Toronto: McClelland & Stewart, 1967), 193–94.

5. Newman, *Caesars of the Wilderness*, 69–70.

6. Elaine Allan Mitchell, "New Evidence on the Mackenzie-McTavish Break," *Canadian Historical Review* 41, no. 1 (March 1960), 45.

7. Ibid., 46.

8. Ibid.

9. Masson, *Les Bourgeois*, vol. 1, 49.

10. Ibid., 50.

11. Quaife, *The John Askin Papers*, vol. II, 274–75.

12. Masson, *Les Bourgeois*, vol. 1, 75–76.

13. Mitchell, "New Evidence," 43–44.

14. Campbell, *McGillivray*, 64.

15. Journals and Correspondence 1795–1802, HBC Record Society, Vol. xxvi, HBC Archives.

16. Campbell, *McGillivray*, 105–6.

17. Ibid., 125.

18. Wallace, *Documents Relating to the North West Company*, 221.

19. François Victoire Malhiot, *A Wisconsin Fur-Traders Journal, 1804–05*. www.marshfield.k12.wi.us/socsci/discovery/malhiot/default.htm, 45–46.

20. Masson, "Journal of Duncan Cameron," in *Les Bourgeois*, vol. 2, 273.

21. Ibid.

22. Gordon, *People of the Fur Trade*, 34–35.

23. Masson, "Journal of Duncan Cameron," in *Les Bourgeois*, vol. 2, 273.

24. Ibid., 274.

25. Ibid., 277–78.

26. Ibid., 295.

27. Masson, *Les Bourgeois*, vol. 1, 47.

28. Jean Morrison. "Some Fur Trade Families from Lake Superior to Rainy Lake," 34.

29. Campbell, *McGillivray*, 111.

CHAPTER 9: DEATHS AND OTHER CHANGES, 1804–11

1. Quaife, *The John Askin Papers*, vol. II, 421.

2. Ibid., 424–25.

3. Wallace, *Documents Relating to the North West Company*, 138.

4. Edgar Andrew Collard, "The Haunted House of Simon McTavish," *Montreal Gazette*, ca. 1970s, Marjorie Wilkins Campbell fonds (P128), McCord Museum.

5. Ibid.

6. R. Harvey Fleming, "The Origin of 'Sir Alexander Mackenzie and Company," *Canadian Historical Review* 9 (1923), 147.

7. Ibid., 148; Fleming includes the text of the New NWC Articles of Agreement and Co-partnership, 148–55.

8. Campbell, *McGillivray*, 138.

9. Ibid., 136.

10. Harmon, *Sixteen Years in the Indian Country*, 105.

11. Campbell, *McGillivray*, 155–56.

12. Podruchny, *Making the Voyageur World*, 143.

13. Ibid., 142–44.

14. Ross Cox, *The Columbia River: Or Scenes and Adventures*, vol. II (London: Henry Colburn & Richard Bentley, 1831), 293.

15. Washington Irving, *Astoria: Or, Anecdotes of an Enterprise Beyond the Rocky Mountains* (Paris: Baudry's European Library, 1836), www.history1700s.com/, 4–5.

16. Ibid., 4.

17. *North West Company Letter Books*, 1792–1824. North West Company Collection (C104) and Marjorie Wilkins Campbell fonds (P128), McCord Museum.

18. Bruce M. White, "Grand Portage as a Trading Post: Patterns of Trade at the Great Carrying Place," (Grand Marais, MN: Grand Portage National Monument, National Parks Service, 2005), 71.

19. Duncan McGillvray's will, dated April 27, 1808, McCord Museum, Marjorie Wilkins Campbell fonds (P128).

20. Campbell, *McGillivray*, 144.

21. Ibid., 147–48.

22. Ibid., 148–49.

23. Quaife, *The John Askin Papers*, vol. II, 673–74.

CHAPTER 10: THE NORTH WEST COMPANY, LORD SELKIRK, AND THE WAR OF 1812

1. Available online at www.ballantynethebrave.com.

2. *Inverness Journal*, June 21, 1811.

3. Ibid., Sept. 20, 1811.

4. Ibid., March 27, 1812.

5. Ibid., May 22, 1812.

6. "Settling Selkirk from the Scots Perspective," *Winnipeg Sun*, posted online Sept. 4, 2012, www.winnipegsun.com/news/archives/2012/9/4.

7. E.E. Rich, "Introduction," in Colin Robertson, *Colin Robertson's Correspondence Book, Sept. 1817 to Sept. 1822*, edited by E.E. Rich (Toronto: Champlain Society, 1939), www.champlainsociety.ca/, xlvi.

8. Campbell, *McGillivray*, 167.

9. Agnes C. Laut, *The Conquest of the Great Northwest*, vol. 2 (New York: Moffat, Yard & Co., 1914; originally published in 1908),http://archive.org/), 118.

10. Campbell, *McGillivray*, 176.

11. J.M. Bumsted, *Fur Trade Wars: The Founding of Western Canada* (Winnipeg, Great Plains Publications, 1999), 86–87.

12. William Wood, *Select British Documents of the Canadian War of 1812*, vol. I (Toronto: The Champlain Society, 1920), http://link.library.utoronto.ca/, 283–84.

13. Campbell, *McGillivray*, 189.

14. Lawrence Barkwell, *Métis Soldiers in the War of 1812*, part I (Saskatoon: Gabriel Dumont Institute of Native Studies and Applied Research, 2012), 1–2.

15. Ibid.

16. Cox, *The Columbia River*, vol. II, 339.

17. Ibid., 338–40.

18. Campbell, *McGillivray*, 194.

19. Ibid., 196.

20. Irene Ternier Gordon, *Tecumseh: Diplomat and Warrior in the War of 1812* (Toronto: James Lorimer & Co., 2009), 72.

21. Dr. C.E. Fryer, "The Patriotic Services of William McKay of Montreal in the War of 1812," McKay Papers, War of 1812–1814 Collection (C177), McCord Museum, 14.

22. Robert Christie, *A History of the Late Province of Lower Canada Parliamentary and Political*, vol. II (Montreal: Richard Worthington, 1866), 41, 231; Fryer, "The Patriotic Services of William McKay," 4, 11–18.

23. Campbell, *McGillivray*, 184.

24. Morrison, *Superior Rendezvous-Place*, 79.

CHAPTER 11: THE ARRIVAL OF THE RED RIVER SETTLERS, 1812–14

1. Brown, *The Big Lonely*.

2. William Douglas, "The Forks Becomes a City," Transactions of the Manitoba Historical Society, Third Series, no. 1 (1944–45), www.mhs.mb.ca/docs/transactions, 6.

3. William Douglas, "New Light on the Old Forts of Winnipeg," Transactions of the Manitoba Historical Society, Third Series, no. (1954–55), www.mhs.mb.ca/docs/transactions, 3. One Douglas article gives the arrival date of the settlers as August 12, the other gives it as August 30.

4. Chester Martin, *Lord Selkirk's Work in Canada* (Oxford: Clarendon Press, 1916), also at http://peel.library.ualberta.ca, 54.

5. Ibid.

6. See Gordon, *People of the Fur Trade* and *The Battle of Seven Oaks* for more information on the clash between the settlers and the Nor'Westers.

7. John Pritchard, *Narratives of John Pritchard Respecting the Aggressions of the North-Company against the Earl of Selkirk's Settlement upon the Red River* (London: John Murray, 1819), http://peel.library.ualberta.ca/, 7–8.

8. Martin, *Lord Selkirk's Work*, 77–78.

9. Pritchard, *Narratives of John Pritchard*, 10. Pritchard went to Montreal before returning to the Red River, where he would spend the rest of his life.

10. Martin, *Lord Selkirk's Work*, 77.

11. Bumsted, *Fur Trade Wars*, 105.

12. John Halkett, *Statement Respecting the Earl of Selkirk's Settlement of Kildonan upon The Red River in North America* (London: J. Brettell, 1817), http://peel.library.ualberta.ca/bibliography/91.html, 15.

13. Ibid., 17.

14. Archibald MacDonald, *Narrative Concerning the Destruction of the Earl of Selkirk'sSettlement upon Red River in the Year 1815* (London: J. Brettell, 1816), http://peel.library.ualberta.ca/, 6.

15. Martin, *Lord Selkirk's Work*, 87–88.

16. Louis Aubrey Wood, *The Red River Colony: A Chronicle of the Beginnings of Manitoba* (Toronto: Glasgow, Brook & Co., 1915), www.gutenberg.org/, 64.

17. Margaret MacLeod and W.L. Morton, *Cuthbert Grant of Grantown* (Toronto: McCelland & Stewart, 1963), 24.

18. Simon McGillivray, *The North West Company in Rebellion: Simon McGillivray's Fort William Notebook, 1815*, edited by Jean Morrison (Thunder Bay: Thunder Bay Historical Museum Society, 1988), 1.

19. Campbell, *McGillivray*, 202.

20. Podruchny, *Making the Voyageur World*, 36.

21. Ibid., 44.

CHAPTER 12: CRISIS AT THE RED RIVER, 1815–16

1. Bumsted, *Fur Trade Wars*, 128.

2. Campbell, *McGillivray*, 217–18.

3. Ibid. 219–20.

4. Martin, *Lord Selkirk's Work*, 93.

5. Ibid.

6. McGillivray, *The North West Company in Rebellion*, July 17.

7. Ibid., July 19.

8. Ibid., July 20.

9. Ibid., July 22.

10. Campbell, *McGillivray*, 224.

11. Laut, *The Conquest of the Great Northwest*, vol. 2, 126–27.

12. Campbell, *McGillivray*, 246.

13. Martin, *Lord Selkirk's Work*, 115–16.

14. Campbell, *McGillivray*. 226–27.

15. Martin, *Lord Selkirk's Work*, 105.

16. For a full account of the battle, see Gordon, *The Battle of Seven Oaks,* 76–82.

17. Campbell, *McGillivray*, 231–32.

CHAPTER 13: THE AFTERMATH OF SEVEN OAKS, 1816–17

1. Brown, *The Big Lonely*.

2. Wood, *Red River Colony*, 118-19.

3. For a history of the de Meuron Swiss regiment and its service with the regular British Army, see http://ccv.northwestcompany.com/demeuron.html.

4. Wood, *The Red River Colony*, 118–28.

5. Campbell, *McGillivray*, 239.

6. Ibid., 240.

7. Bumsted, *Fur Trade Wars*, 160.

8. The following account is based on Gaspard Adolph Fauché, "Account of the Transactions at Fort William, on Lake Superior, in August 1816" (Westminister: Queen Square, 1817), http://peel.library.ualberta.ca/, 67–70.

9. Wood, *The Red River Colony*, 125–27.

10. Morrison, *Superior Rendezvous-Place*, 91–92.

11. Ibid.

12. Letter. Angus Shaw to James Fraser, October 14, 1816, National Records of Scotland GD45/3/17.

13. Ibid.

14. Ibid.

15. Martin, *Lord Selkirk's Work*, 129.

16. Bumsted, *Fur Trade Wars*, 204.

17. Martin, *Lord Selkirk's Work*, 119.

18. F.L. Barron, "Victimizing His Lordship: Lord Selkirk and the Upper Canadian Courts," *Manitoba History* 7 (Spring 1984), www.mhs.mb.ca/docs/mb_history/07/victimizinglordship.shtml, 3.

19. Ibid., 6.

20. Martin, *Lord Selkirk's Work*, 148.

21. Campbell, *McGillivray*, 265–66.

22. Ibid., 268.

23. Ibid.

CHAPTER 14: THE NORTH WEST COMPANY AND THE PACIFIC TRADE, 1795–1815

1. Brown, *The Big Lonely*.

2. "Nor'westers and Astorians," www.3rd1000.com/history3/era6.htm.

3. Letter, Alexander Henry to Simon McTavish, Nov. 23, 1794, F. 3/1 folio 212, HBC Archives.

4. Letter, James Hallowell to Simon McTavish, May 22, 1795, F.3/1 folios 227–28, HBC Archives.

5. Ibid., folio 235.

6. Morrison, *Superior Rendezvous-Place,* 70.

7. Ibid.

8. Bumsted, *Fur Trade Wars*, 27.

9. Nathaniel Atcheson (attributed), *On the Origin and Progress of the North-West Company of Canada, with a History of the Fur Trade* (London: Cox, Son, & Baylis, 1811), 11, 13–14.

10. Ibid., 17.

11. H. Lloyd Keith, "Voyage of the *Isaac Todd*," *Oregon Historical Quarterly* 109, no. 4 (Winter 2008), 3.

12. A licence granted by a sovereign to a subject to fit out an armed vessel and employ it in the capture of merchant ships belonging to an enemy country's subjects.

13. Keith, "Voyage of the *Isaac Todd*," 4.

14. Ibid., 5.
15. Ibid., 17.

CHAPTER 15: ATHABASCA COUNTRY AND
THE LAST YEARS OF THE NORTH WEST COMPANY, 1818–20
1. Robertson, *Colin Robertson's Correspondence Book*, 72–73.
2. Douglas, "New Light on the Old Forts of Winnipeg," 38.
3. Ibid., 38–39.
4. Ibid., 39.
5. Robertson, *Colin Robertson's Correspondence Book*, 124.
6. Ibid., 128.
7. Ibid.
8. Ibid., xvi–vii, xxi.
9. Ibid., 138–39.
10. Simon McGillivray Jr. Diary 1820–21, Simon McGillivray Jr. fonds, MG19-A33, R7893-0-9-E, Library and Archives Canada, 1.
11. Ibid., 3–4.
12. Ibid, 9.
13. Ibid., 33.
14. Ibid., 38.
15. *Montreal Gazette*, February 4, 1818.
16. John J. Bigsby, *The Shoe and the Canoe* (New York: Paladin Press, 1969; first published 1850 by Chapman and Hall), 108–9.
17. Ibid., 112.

CHAPTER 16: AMALGAMATION, 1820–21
1. Brown, *The Big Lonely*.
2. Wallace, *Documents Relating to the North West Company*, 317–18.
3. Campbell, *McGillivray*, 288.
4. Wallace, *Documents Relating to the North West Company*, 320.
5. Ibid., 322–23.
6. Campbell, *McGillivray*, 292.
7. Wallace, *Documents Relating to the North West Company*, 327.
8. Ibid., 374.
9. Campbell, *McGillivray*, 294.
10. Ibid., 295–96.
11. Ibid., 296.
12. Campbell, *The North West Company*, 272.
13. Robertson, *Colin Robertson's Correspondence Book*, 163–64.
14. Nicholas Garry, *Diary of Nicholas Garry, deputy-governor of the Hudson's Bay Company from 1822–1835* (Ottawa: Royal Society of Canada, 1900), also at http://peel.library.ualberta.ca/bibliography/142.html, 116–117.
15. Ibid.
16. Ibid., 83–84.
17. Ibid., 116, 118.
18. Ibid., 133–34.
19. Ibid., 140.
20. Ibid., 144–45.
21. Ibid., 152.
22. Ibid., 165–67.
23. R. Harvey Fleming, ed. *Minutes of Council Northern Department of Rupert Land, 1821–31* (Toronto: The Champlain Society, 1940), http://link.library.utoronto.ca/, 391.
24. Ibid.
25. Ibid., 391–92.
26. Wallace, *Documents Relating to the North West Company*, 328.

27. Ibid., 329.

28. Ibid.

CHAPTER 17: WINDING DOWN, 1822–25

1. Campbell, *McGillivray*, 313.

2. Ibid., 314.

3. Jennifer S.H. Brown, "Woman as Centre and Symbol in the Emergence of Métis Communities," *Canadian Journal of Native Studies* 3, no. 1 (1983), www2.brandonu.ca/library/CJNS/3.1/brown.pdf, 43–44.

4. Gilbert Malcolm Sproat, "Career of a Scotch Boy," edited by Madge Wolfenden, *British Columbia Historical Quarterly* 18, nos. 3 and 4 (July–October 1954), www.library.ubc.ca/, 153–54.

5. Ibid., 155

6. MacLeod and Morton, *Cuthbert Grant of Grantown*, 79.

7. Ibid., 86.

8. Fleming, *Minutes of Council Northern Department*, 407–8.

9. Ibid., 409.

10. Campbell, *McGillivray*, 322–23.

11. Wallace, *Documents Relating to the North West Company*, 32.

12. Auction by Christie's, McGillivray family fonds (P100), McCord Museum.

13. Campbell, *McGillivray*, 321.

14. Ibid., 317–18

15. Ibid., 329–30.

16. Wallace, *Documents Relating to the North West Company*, 376.

EPILOGUE: THE LAST LAIRD OF THE NORTH WEST COMPANY

1. Wallace, *Documents Relating to the North West Company*, 371–72.

2. Ibid., 372.

3. Ibid., 334.

4. Ibid., 27.

5. Wallace, *Documents Relating to the North West Company*, 35–36.

6. MacLeod and Morton, *Cuthbert Grant*, 97–98.

7. Campbell, *McGillivray*, vii.

8. Irving, *Astoria*, 5.

≋ SELECTED BIBLIOGRAPHY ≋

The following resources provided important information about William McGillivray and the North West Company. I have provided annotations for significant sources where this information is helpful.

BOOKS

Atcheson, Nathaniel (attributed). *On the Origin and Progress of the North-West Company of Canada, with a History of the Fur Trade*. London: Cox, Son, & Baylis, 1811. http://peel. library.ualberta.ca/.

Barkwell, Lawrence. *Métis Soldiers in the War of 1812*. Part I. Saskatoon: Gabriel Dumont Institute of Native Studies and Applied Research, 2012.

Bigsby, John J. *The Shoe and the Canoe*. New York: Paladin Press, 1969. First published 1850 by Chapman and Hall. [Description of life in Montreal and a party at the McGillivray home ca. 1820.]

Bumsted, J.M. *Fur Trade Wars: The Founding of Western Canada*. Winnipeg: Great Plains Publications, 1999.

Campbell, Marjorie Wilkins. *McGillivray: Lord of the Northwest*. Toronto: Clarke, Irwin, 1962.

———. *The North West Company*. Vancouver: Douglas & McIntyre, 1973. [Includes the NWC's view regarding amalgamation with the HBC]

Cox, Ross. *The Columbia River: Or Scenes and Adventures*. Vol. II. London: Henry Colburn & Richard Bentley, 1831. [Description of Fort William and the Corps of Canadian Voyageurs during the War of 1812.]

Davidson, Gordon Charles. *The North West Company*. Berkeley: University of California Press, 1918.

Duckworth, Harry W. *The English River Notebook: A North West Company Journal and Account Book of 1786*. Montreal: McGill-Queen's University Press, 1990.

Fauché, Gaspard Adolph. "Account of the Transactions at Fort William, on Lake Superior, in August 1816." Westminister: Queen Square, 1817. http://peel.library.ualberta.ca/.

Fleming, R. Harvey, ed. *Minutes of Council Northern Department of Rupert Land, 1821–31*. Toronto: The Champlain Society, 1940. http://link.library.utoronto.ca/. [George Simpson as HBC governor.]

Franchère, Gabriel. *Adventure at Astoria 1810–1814*. Translated and edited by Hoyt C.

Franchère, Norman: University of Oklahoma Press, 1967. [Events during the War of 1812.]

Fraser, Esther. *The Canadian Rockies: Early Travels and Exploration*. Edmonton: Hurtig, 1969. [Duncan McGillivray's career as an explorer.]

Garry, Nicholas. *Diary of Nicholas Garry, deputy-governor of the Hudson's Bay Company from 1822–1835*. Ottawa: Royal Society of Canada, 1900. http://peel.library.ualberta.ca/. [Description of the voyage made by Garry and Simon McGillivray to implement the amalgamation of the NWC and HBC.]

Gates, Charles M. ed. *Five Fur Traders of the Northwest: Being the Narrative of Peter Pond and the Diaries of John MacDonell, Archibald N. McLeod, Hugh Faries and Thomas Connor*. Introduction by Grace Lee Nute. Minneapolis: University of Minnesota Press, 1933. [Description of fur-trade life by MacDonell.]

Gordon, Irene Ternier. *The Battle of Seven Oaks and the Violent Birth of the Red River Settlement*. Canmore: Altitude Publishing, 2005.

———. *Tecumseh: Diplomat and Warrior in the War of 1812*. Toronto: Lorimer, 2009. [Communications during the War of 1812.]

Halkett, John. *Statement Respecting the Earl of Selkirk's Settlement of Kildonan upon The Red River in North America*. London: J. Brettell, 1817. http://peel.library.ualberta.ca/.

Hargrave, J.J. *Red River*. Ottawa: Minister of Agriculture and Statistics, 1871, reprinted 1977.

Harmon, Daniel Williams. *Sixteen Years in the Indian Country: the Journal of Daniel Williams Harmon*. Edited by W. Kaye Lamb. Toronto: Macmillan, 1957. [Description of fur-trade life at Fort William.]

Henry, Alexander (the Elder). *Travels and Adventures in Canada and the Indian Territories between the Years 1760 and 1776*. New York: I. Riley, 1809. www.canadiana.org.

Innis, Harold A. *The Fur Trade in Canada*. Rev. ed. Toronto: University of Toronto Press, 1956.

———. *Peter Pond: Fur Trader and Adventurer*. Toronto: Irwin & Gordon, 1930. www.gutenberg.ca/.

Innis, Mary Quayle, ed. *Mrs. Simcoe's Diary*. Toronto: Macmillan, 1965. [Life in Montreal ca. 1791.]

Irving, Washington. *Astoria: Or, Anecdotes of an Enterprise Beyond the Rocky Mountains*. Paris: Baudry's European Library, 1836. www.history1700s.com/. [Description of life at Fort William.]

Kalm, Peter. *Travels into North America*. Vols. 2 and 3. Translated by John Reinhold Forster. Cambridge: Cambridge University Press, 2011. First published in London by Eyres, 1771. [Winter travel in Quebec.]

Landmann, George Thomas. *Adventures and Recollections of Colonel Landmann Late of the Corps of Royal Engineers*. Vol. 1. London: Colburn & Co., 1852. http://babel.hathitrust.org/. [Winter travel and Beaver Club social events in Quebec.]

Laut, Agnes C. *The Conquest of the Great Northwest*. Vols. 1 and 2. New York: Moffat, Yard & Co., 1914. Originally published in 1908. http://archive.org/.

Lighthall, William W. *Montreal after 250 Years*. Montreal: Grafton, 1892. www.gutenberg.ca/. [Describes NWC buildings and the homes of prominent Nor'Westers.]

MacDonald, Archibald. *Narrative Concerning the Destruction of the Earl of Selkirk's Settlement upon Red River in the Year 1815*. London: J. Brettell, 1816. http://peel.library.ualberta.ca/.

MacGregor, J.G. *Peter Fidler: Canada's Forgotten Explorer 1769–1822*. Calgary: Fifth House, 1998. [Life at the Red River Settlement.]

Mackenzie, Alexander, *Voyages from Montreal on the River St. Laurence through the Continent of North America*. London: T. Cadell, 1801. http://peel.library.ualberta.ca/.

MacLeod, Margaret, and W.L. Morton. *Cuthbert Grant of Grantown*. Toronto: McCelland & Stewart, 1963.

Malhiot, François Victoire. *A Wisconsin Fur-Traders Journal, 1804–05*. www.marshfield.k12.wi.us/socsci/discovery/malhiot/default.htm. [Fur-trade life.]

Marchildon, Greg, and Sid Robinson. *Canoeing the Churchill: A Practical Guide to the Historic Voyageur Highway*. Regina: Canadian Plains Research Center, 2002.

Martin, Chester. *Lord Selkirk's Work in Canada*. Oxford: Clarendon Press, 1916. http://peel.library.ualberta.ca/.

Masson, L.R., ed. *Les Bourgeois de la Compagnie du Nord-Ouest*. 2 vols. Quebec: A. Coté et Cie., 1889–90. http://archive.org/. [Information about Roderick McKenzie and Duncan Cameron.]

McGillivray, Duncan. *The Journal of Duncan M'Gillivray of the North West Company at Fort George on the Saskatchewan, 1794–5*. Edited by A.S. Morton. Toronto: Macmillan, 1929. http://peel.library.ualberta.ca/.

McGillivray, Simon. *The North West Company in Rebellion: Simon McGillivray's Fort William Notebook, 1815*. Edited by Jean Morrison. Thunder Bay: Thunder Bay Historical Museum Society, 1988.

Morrison, Jean. "Some Fur Trade Families from Lake Superior to Rainy Lake." In *Lake Superior to Rainy Lake: Three Centuries of Fur Trade History*. Edited by Jean Morrison. Thunder Bay: Thunder Bay Historical Museum Society, 2003.

————. *Superior Rendezvous-Place: Fort William in the Canadian Fur Trade*. Toronto: National Heritage Books, 2001.

Morse, Eric W. *Fur Trade Canoe Routes of Canada: Then and Now*. Ottawa: National and Historic Parks Branch, 1969.

Newman, Peter C. *Caesars of the Wilderness*. Markham: Penguin Books, 1987.

Nute, Grace Lee. *The Voyageur*. St. Paul: Minnesota Historical Society, 1955.

Podruchny, Carolyn. *Making the Voyageur World: Travelers and Traders in the North American Fur Trade*. Toronto: University of Toronto Press, 2006.

Pritchard, John. *Narratives of John Pritchard Respecting the Aggressions of the North-Company against the Earl of Selkirk's Settlement upon the Red River*. London: John Murray, 1819. http://peel.library.ualberta.ca/.

Quaife, Milo M., ed. *The John Askin Papers*. 2 vols. Detroit: Detroit Library Commission, 1928–1931. http://quod.lib.umich.edu/.

Rich, E.E. *The Fur Trade and the Northwest to 1857*. Toronto: McClelland & Stewart, 1967.

Robertson, Colin. *Colin Robertson's Correspondence Book, Sept. 1817 to Sept. 1822*. Edited by E.E. Rich. Toronto: Champlain Society, 1939. www.champlainsociety.ca/.

Ross, Alexander. *The Fur Hunters of the Far West: A Narrative of Adventures in the Oregon and Rocky Mountains*. 2 vols. London: Smith, Elder & Co., 1855. http://eco.canadiana.ca/. [Grand Portage.]

Simpson, George. *Journal of Occurrences in the Athabasca Department, 1820 and 1821*. Edited by E.E. Rich. Toronto: The Champlain Society, 1938. Also at http://link.library.utoronto.ca/.

Toye, William. *The St. Lawrence*. Toronto: Oxford University Press, 1959.

Wallace, W. Stewart, ed. *Documents Relating to the North West Company*. Toronto: The Champlain Society, 1934. www.champlainsociety.ca/.

Weld, Isaac. *Travels though the States of North America and the Provinces of Upper and Lower Canada, During the Years 1795, 1796, and 1797*. London: John Stockdale, 1799. http://eco.canadiana.ca/.

Wood, Louis Aubrey. *The Red River Colony: A Chronicle of the Beginnings of Manitoba*. Toronto: Glasgow, Brook & Co., 1915. Also at www.gutenberg.org/.

Wood, William. *Select British Documents of the Canadian War of 1812*. Vol. I. Toronto: The Champlain Society, 1920. http://link.library.utoronto.ca/.

ARTICLES

Barron, F.L. "Victimizing His Lordship: Lord Selkirk and the Upper Canadian Courts." *Manitoba History* 7 (Spring 1984): 14–22. www.mhs.mb.ca/docs/mb_history/07/victimizinglordship.shtml.

Brown, Jennifer S.H. "Woman as Centre and Symbol in the Emergence of Métis Communities." *Canadian Journal of Native Studies* 3, no. 1 (1983), 39–46. www2.brandonu.ca/library/CJNS/3.1/brown.pdf. [Discusses McGillivray's views regarding the Métis]

Brown, Michael, ed. "Transnational Dimensions." In *Layers of Power: Societies and Institutions in Europe*. Edited by Saúl Martínez Bermejo. Pisa: Pisa University Press, 2010. http://ehlee.humnet.unipi.it/books5/1/06.pdf. [Description of NWC fur marketing in Europe.]

Calverley, Dorthea. "The Voyageurs, the Backbone of the Fur Trade." www.calverley.ca/.

Douglas, William. "The Forks Becomes a City." Transactions of the Manitoba Historical Society, Third Series, no. 1 (1944–45). www.mhs.mb.ca/docs/transactions.

————. "New Light on the Old Forts of Winnipeg." Transactions of the Manitoba Historical Society, Series 3, (1954-55). www.mhs.mb.ca/docs/transactions.

Fleming, R. Harvey, "The Origin of Sir Alexander Mackenzie and Company." *Canadian Historical Review* 9 (1923): 137–55.

Keith, H. Lloyd. "Voyage of the *Isaac Todd*," *Oregon Historical Quarterly* 109, no. 4 (Winter 2008): 568–90. [NWC fur trade in China and on the Pacific coast.]

Mitchell, Elaine Allan. "New Evidence on the Mackenzie-McTavish Break." *Canadian Historical Review* 41, no. 1 (March 1960): 41–7.

———. "The North West Company Agreement of 1795." *Canadian Historical Review* 36, no. 2 (June 1955): 131–35.

"Nor'Westers and Astorians." www.3rd1000.com/history3/era6.htm.

Nute, Grace Lee. "A British Legal Case and Old Grand Portage." *Minnesota History* 21 (June 1940): 117–48. http://collections.mnhs.org/.

Senior, Dr. Elinor Kyte. "Christmas Eve in Montreal 1783—A Bleak Mid-Winter." *Loyalist Gazette* 24 (June 1986): 15–16. http://www.uelac.org/.

Sproat, Gilbert Malcolm. "Career of a Scotch Boy." Edited by Madge Wolfenden. *British Columbia Historical Quarterly* 18, nos. 3 and 4 (July–October 1954): 133–238. www.library.ubc.ca/. [Account of the first joint celebration between HBC and NWC employees after 1821 at York Factory.]

White, Bruce M. "Grand Portage as a Trading Post: Patterns of Trade at the Great Carrying Place." Grand Marais, MN: Grand Portage National Monument, National Parks Service, 2005.

ARCHIVAL SOURCES

HBC Archives, Winnipeg, Manitoba:

Journals and Correspondence 1795–1802. HBC Record Society, Vol. XXVI.

Letter, Alexander Henry to Simon McTavish, Nov. 23, 1794, F. 3/1 folio 212.

Letter, James Hallowell to Simon McTavish, November 17, 1794, F.3/1 folio 208.

Letter, James Hallowell to Simon McTavish, May 22, 1795. F.3/1 folios 227–28, 235.

"Richards, John (Captain)." fl. HBC, NWC 1782–1803.

McCord Museum, Montreal, Quebec:

The Beaver Club Minute Book, Beaver Club fonds (P305).

Collard, Edgar Andrew. "The Haunted House of Simon McTavish." *Montreal Gazette*, ca. 1970s. Marjorie Wilkins Campbell fonds (P128).

Fryer, Dr. C. E. "The Patriotic Services of William McKay of Montreal in the War of 1812." McKay Papers, War of 1812–1814 Collection (C177).

Gingras, Larry. *The Beaver Club Jewels.* Canadian Numismatic Research Society, 1972. Beaver Club Collection (P305).

Inverness Journal. Miscellaneous articles 1811, 1812. Marjorie Wilkins Campbell fonds (P128).

Mackay, William. *Sidelights on Highland History.* Inverness: Northern Counties Newspaper and Print and Publishing Company, 1925. Marjorie Wilkins Campbell fonds (P128).

North West Company Letter Books, 1792–1824. North West Company Collection (C104) and Marjorie Wilkins Campbell fonds (P128).

Other:

Letter. Angus Shaw to James Fraser, October 14, 1816, National Records of Scotland GD45/3/17.

OTHER RESOURCES

Brown, Rodney. *The Big Lonely.* Starsilk Records, 2004, compact disc.

———. *North Land.* Starsilk Records, 2009, compact disc.

Dictionary of Canadian Biography Online. www.biographi.ca/.

≡ INDEX ≋

⇒ ACKNOWLEDGEMENTS ⇐

THANK YOU TO the following people and organizations for their assistance in making this book possible:

Editor Lesley Reynolds, who did her usual excellent job in preparing my manuscript for publication.

My husband, Don, who has always offered me encouragement.

The Jean Morrison Canadian Fur Trade Library staff at the Fort William Historical Park in Thunder Bay, Ontario.

McCord Museum of Canadian History in Montreal, especially Nora Hague, senior cataloguer, and the staff who assisted me in ordering illustrations for this book.

Hudson Bay Archives in Winnipeg, especially archivists Mandy Malazdrewich and Denise Jones.

Library and Archives Canada staff who assisted me in ordering illustrations for this book.

Rodney Brown, Thunder Bay musician and songwriter with a special interest in the history of his hometown and William McGillivray. Rodney generously gave me permission to use some of his lyrics to introduce chapters of this book.

≡ ABOUT THE AUTHOR ≡

Irene Ternier Gordon was raised on a grain farm in west-central Saskatchewan and has lived along the historic Assiniboine River just west of Winnipeg since 1989. She has been interested in western Canadian history since she was eleven years old and first read the children's historical novels written by Manitoban Olive Knox. She began her writing career in 1998, after working as a teacher-librarian for fifteen years. When she is not writing, she is an avid traveller and especially enjoys going someplace warm for a couple of weeks every winter.

The Laird of Fort William is Irene's eighth book. For more information about Irene or her work, please go to www.ireneterniergordon.ca or contact her at author@ireneterniergordon.ca.